Martin Sherlock

Letters from an English Traveller

Martin Sherlock

Letters from an English Traveller

ISBN/EAN: 9783744768009

Printed in Europe, USA, Canada, Australia, Japan

Cover: Foto ©ninafisch / pixelio.de

More available books at **www.hansebooks.com**

LETTERS

FROM

AN ENGLISH TRAVELLER

[MARTIN SHERLOCK, Esq.]

[Price Two Shillings and Six Pence.]

FROM

AN ENGLISH TRAVELLER

[MARTIN SHERLOCK, Esq.]

TRANSLATED FROM THE FRENCH ORIGINAL
PRINTED AT GENEVA AND PARIS.

WITH NOTES.

A NEW EDITION, REVISED AND CORRECTED.

Rien n'eſt beau que le vrai, le vrai ſeul eſt aimable.
BOILEAU.

Nothing is beautiful but Truth,
And Truth alone is lovely.

LONDON,
PRINTED FOR J. NICHOLS, T. CADELL,
P. ELMSLY, H. PAYNE, AND N. CONANT.
MDCCLXXX.

TO THE RIGHT HONOURABLE

THE EARL OF BRISTOL,

BISHOP OF DERRY.

My Lord,

DEDICATIONS, in general, are so fulsome and heavy, that they disgust even the persons to whom they are addressed: As for me, I will not praise you, because every one praises you: I have seen many countries; and in every town where you have resided, I have heard a repetition of the same elogiums on the goodness of your heart, the sweetness of your manners, and the charms of your wit. The most respectable and the most accomplished persons were those who praised you most. I beg your Lordship to accept this tribute as a proof of my esteem, and to believe that I am, with the most sincere attachment, and with the most profound respect,

My Lord,

Your Lordship's most humble

And most-obedient servant,

MARTIN SHERLOCK.

PREFACE.

I could present to the publick two hundred letters; I offer them twenty, because I thought I should shew them more respect by publishing a hundred pages, which they might read twice, than by printing a thousand, of which they would never read half. As to *agrémens* of style, none will be found, for it is an Englishman who writes: In a plain style will be found some ideas and truth.

The notes between [ ] are added by the translator.

The author paſſing through Potſdam ſent this book to the King. His Majeſty honoured him with the following anſwer.

Monſieur de Sherlock, Je vous remercie du livre que vous venez de M'adreſſer. Il a trouvé l'accueil qu'il mérite. Je deſire même de revoir ſon auteur, & vous vous rendrez pour cet effet chez Moi, demain vers les onze heures avant-midi. Ce ſera M. Général Major Comte de Goërtz qui a ordre de vous y conduire & de vous preſenter, & ſur ce Je prie Dieu qu'il vous ait, Monſieur de Sherlock, en ſa ſainte & digne garde.

Potſdam, ce 19 Juillet, 1779.   FREDERIC.

CONTENTS.

LETTER I. P. 1.

CHARACTER of the King of Pruſſia. Its two parts. The Queen. Princeſs Amelia. A ſcene for Rubens. Coriolanus. Frederick not only great, but good.

LETTER II. P. 8.

Review at Potſdam. Battle deſcribed. Pictures from Taſſo. King's perſon and manner.

LETTER III. P. 15.

Another battle. The King's apartments. A Swiſs wit. The author preſented to the King. Lord Chatham. Dutcheſs of Kingston.

LETTER IV. P. 19.

The Great Frederick's œconomy and generoſity. Anecdote of a French count. Elogium on the King-poet. Compariſon of him with Horace. Extract from his epiſtle on travelling.

CONTENTS.

LETTER V. P. 26.

King of Pruſſia's love of mankind. His ode on war. His art of war his maſter-piece. His addreſs to young ſoldiers.

LETTER. VI. P. 35.

Beauties of Saxony. King of Pruſſia and Veſuvius. Elogium of Corregio. Corregio and Raphael compared. Famous ſaying of the former. Monteſquieu's application of it to himſelf.

LETTER VII. P. 45.

Agreeableneſs of Vienna. Beauty and accompliſhments of the ladies. Counteſs of Dirheim. Princeſſes Charles Lichtenſtein and Lignoſki. Counteſſes Paar, Wurmbrand, Buquoy, Loſs, Bergen, and Degenfield. Baroneſs de Rheiſhach. Prince Kaunitz. The Pope's Nuncio. Sir Robert Keith. Baron de Breteuil.

LETTER VIII. P. 53.

German and Italian theatres. La Sacco. Proceſſion of the Knights of the Golden Fleece. The courſe of ſledges. Dreſſes of the ladies and their knights. Prince Kaunitz's anti-chamber.

CONTENTS.

LETTER IX. P. 57.

Metastasio. His excellences, education, and studies. His superiority to Dante, Ariosto, Marini, and Tasso. Beauties and faults of the Jerusalem Delivered. Perfection of Aminta.

LETTER X. P. 65.

Singularity and sameness of Holland. Its cardinal virtue and deities. Its school of painting. Mechanism of the art. A saying of Lewis XIV. Bad taste of the modern French. Rubens. Great merit of Sir Joseph Yorke. His magnificent supper.

LETTER XI. P. 70.

Grandeur and gloominess of Rome. Their causes. The Pope and Cardinals. Cardinal de Bernis. The prevailing studies. The Roman women. The national pride and dissimulation. Resemblance of modern and ancient Rome. Distinction between the women of Rome and Naples.

LETTER XII. P. 77.

Summit of Vesuvius. Court of the Apollo of Belvedere. Superiority of the Greeks. Elogium of the Apollo. The Apollos of Bernini and Bouchardon.

CONTENTS.

don. The Laocoon. Story of Michael Angelo. Opinion of Pouſſin and Monteſquieu.

LETTER XIII. P. 88.

Loſs of a favourite dog. Lamentation. Too much of nothing.

LETTER XIV. P. 91.

Beauties of Naples. Objects in view. Poſilipo and Veſuvius. The Volcano. Portici. The gulph. Iſle of Caprea.

LETTER. XV. P. 95.

Academia de Cavalieri; Rudeneſs of a young French Marquis. The French national character. France and England the firſt nations. A French officer. Dialogue. The Abbé Galiani. The Duke della Torre, and his ſons.

LETTER XVI. P. 102.

Barbariſm and civility of the Neapolitans. Sirens and Circes. Reſemblance between the Ruſſians and the Neapolitans. Their women. A Muſico and a Dutcheſs. Train of lovers. Dog recovered.

CONTENTS.

LETTER XVII. P. 108.

Saying of the King of Spain. His Sicilian Majesty. Caserta. Sir William Hamilton. His letters and character. Death of the Prince. Queen's affliction. Affecting circumstances.

LETTER XVIII. P. 112.

The Tiber and Augustus. Horace and Virgil. The Great Frederick. His address. His triple immortality. His ode on Glory. Extracts.

LETTER XIX. P. 116.

Agreeable French houses at Rome. Cardinal de Bernis's assemblies. Bailiff de la Brilliante's dinners. His service of china. Its capture by the English. Grand assembly of Monseigneur de Bayanne. His character. His brother. Marchioness de Bocca-Paduli. Lady Louisa Nugent. Her extraordinary accomplishments and true portrait. Three nations her admirers.

LETTER XX. P. 123.

Blindness of the Italians. Their idolatry of Dante and Ariosto. The author's sentiments. His publication in Italian. Its reception. Approbation of the Count de Bianconi. Sonnet to him by the Abbé Scarpelli. His self-love increased.

LETTER XXI. P. 134.

Excellence of Shakspeare. Appeal to Longinus, Horace, and Boileau. Arguments in favour of Shakspeare. His faults and beauties contrasted with those of Dante. A walk in St. Peter's. A Frenchman, a Pole, and an Englishman. Shakspeare and Michael Angelo. Quotation from Longinus. Carlo Maratti, Rubens, and Corregio.

LETTER XXII. P. 146.

Passage of the Alps. Ridiculousness of Nature. French concert. Another volume of letters. Prince Ernest of Mecklenburgh-Strelitz. Venice the Athens of Italy. The Venuses of Titian and Medicis.

LETTER XXIII. P. 150.

Introduction to Voltaire. His nephew. Beautiful prospect. Dialogue.

LETTER XXIV. P. 158.

Dinner at Ferney. Father Adam. Second dialogue. Bust of Newton.

LET-

LETTER XXV. P. 165.

Particulars of Voltaire. His employments and ambitions. His village. His dress. His church and tomb.

LETTER XXVI. P. 169.

La Bruyere's warning to an author. The author's consciousness of his defects.

LETTER XXVII. P. 171.

Objects should be viewed on the fair side. The contrary system pursued and adopted. Advice to travellers. Conclusion. One point in which all nations agree.

LETTERS

LETTERS

FROM AN

ENGLISH TRAVELLER.

LETTER I.

BERLIN, *Oct.* 10, 1777.

THE King of Pruſſia is every where known as a great king, a great warrior, and a great politician; but he is not every where known as a great poet and a *good man*. Marcus Aurelius, Horace, Machiavel, and Cæſar, have been his models, and he has almoſt ſurpaſſed them all. I have never heard of a human being that was perfect; and this monarch alſo has his faults; but *take him for all in all*, he is the greateſt man that ever exiſted.

At the beginning of his life he publiſhed his Anti-Machiavel, and this was one of the completeſt ſtrokes of Machiavelifm that ever he made. It was a letter of recommendation of himſelf that he wrote to Europe at the inſtant when he had formed the plan of ſeizing Sileſia.

To his ſubjects he is the juſteſt of ſovereigns: to his neighbours he is the moſt dangerous of heroes; his neighbours ſhudder at him, his ſubjects adore him. The Pruſſians are proud of their Great Frederick, as they always ſtyle him. They ſpeak of him with the utmoſt freedom, and

at

at the same time that they criticise severely *some* of his tastes, they give him the highest elogiums. He was told that some one had spoken ill of him. He asked if that person had 100,000 men? He was answered, No. 'Very well,' said the king, 'I can do 'nothing; if he had 100,000 men, 'I would declare war against him.'

Of all the characters of the present age, that of this prince has been the most mistaken; and the reason is, that two parts of his character have been confounded, and only one judgement formed on two points, each of which requires a separate opinion. The King of Prussia has occasioned the death of some thousands of men; and the King of Prussia is a merciful, tender, and compassionate prince. This seems a contradiction; and it is a certain truth. He muſt firſt be conſidered as a conqueror, where it is not permitted to liſten to the voice of humanity. When heroiſm is out of the queſtion, we muſt examine the man. It will be ſaid that this is a ſubtlety. I deny it, and appeal to hiſtory: What clemency more acknowledged than that of Julius Cæſar? What conqueror has ſhed more blood?

I own to you, that, when I entered Pruſſia, I had ſome prejudices againſt the king: theſe are the reaſons that made me change my opinion.

He was forced to marry the queen; and though he has never lived with her, ſhe loves him, becauſe he has always treated her with reſpect, and has always ſhewn her many little attentions.

tentions. She has a palace at Berlin, and another at Schenhaufen, where she paſſes the ſummer. Her court, which she holds twice a week, is brilliant and numerous, becauſe it is known that the king is pleaſed with the reſpect that is shewn her. She has ſome heſitation in her ſpeech; but she is the beſt princeſs in the world, and the king eſteems her highly.

The princeſs Amelia is oppreſſed with infirmities and years. She has loſt the uſe of one arm and the ſight of one eye. She has wit and an improved underſtanding; and the king never goes to Berlin for five hours but he paſſes three with his ſiſter.

The following incident was related to me by her Royal Highneſs the reigning

reigning Dutchefs of Brunfwick*: While fhe had the fmall-pox, the king went to fee her; fhe was thought to be in great danger; he threw himfelf on his knees by her bed-fide, kiffed her hand, and bathed it with tears. What a moment for a Rubens to paint the moft formidable monarch in Europe paying this tribute of fenfibility to a fifter whom he loved! And what a companion for the picture of Coriolanus †, at the inftant when that haughty Roman was facrificing to an emotion of tendernefs his life, his glory, and his revenge!

[* Styled by Dr. Moore, in his late 'View of Society and Manners in France,' &c. the king's favourite fifter.]

† The king has befpoke this picture; and it is now almoft finifhed by the celebrated Battoni at Rome.

Man

Man is a difcontented animal; he loves to complain: the king's fubjects complain of taxes, and I have never feen any fubjects who do not complain of taxes. The Pruffians complain lefs than any others, and the reafon is evident: the government is even and fteady, and the weight of the taxes does not alter, as in other countries; it is always the fame. Men every where take pleafure in fpeaking ill of their fovereign: God knows there never was a better king than ours, and his fubjects fpeak ill of him every day. To me therefore it is a very ftrong proof that the Great Frederick is good, that his fubjects fay little ill of him, and much in his commendation. But here is another proof much ftronger: he has never put a man to death*; and when I tell you that he lives without guards, I fancy you will allow that to be a proof of his feeling inwardly that he has never done an unjuſt action.

LETTER II.

BERLIN.

PLUTARCH and Shakſpeare have ſhewn great men in their night-caps and ſlippers. I cannot ſhew you his Pruſſian Majeſty in his night-cap, for he never wears one; he acquired a habit in his youth of ſleeping bare-headed in order to harden himſelf. Nor has he any ſlippers, for as ſoon

[* The author muſt doubtleſs mean in time of peace, by the civil ſword. In war, in battle, how many thouſands have been put to death by him and his military executioners!]

as he leaves his bed he puts on his boots. It is known that he rifes at four, that he goes to bed at nine, that he procraftinates nothing, that he is fond of jefting, that he eats a great deal of fruit, that he plays on the flute every evening, that he paffes moft of his time at Sans-fouci in his old boots, and that he governs Europe.

I faw him three times; the two firft were at the review at Potfdam; the fun fhone bright, and 40,000 men were divided into two bodies to form a battle. An old general told me in the evening at fupper at the Prince Royal's, that, if I had been in an engagement, I fhould not have had fo perfect an idea of a battle as that which I had received. To pretend to give you a description of it would be as absurd as impossible: read those of Homer and Tasso; all that they say is true, especially this stanza:

In tanto il sol, che ne' celesti campi
Va più sempre avanzando, e in alto ascende,
L'armi percote, e ne trae fiamme, e lampi
Tremuli e chiari, onde le viste offende.
L'aria par di faville intorno avampi,
E quasi d'alto incendio in forma splende;
E co' fieri nitriti il suono accorda
Del ferro scosso, e le campagne assorda. I. 73.

Mean time the sun above th' horizon gains
The rising circuit of th' ethereal plains;
The polish'd arms reflect his dazzling light,
And strike with flashing rays the aching sight.
Thick and more thick the sparkling gleams aspire,
Till all the champain seems to glow with fire;
While mingled clamours echo through the meads,
The clash of arms, the neigh of trampling steeds.
Hoole.

But

But it is one of those things which must be seen to have an idea of it. There are a thousand circumstances which produce an effect on the spectator, and none on paper. The instant of my seeing the enemy's army appear at a distance (for that of the king was on the ground before my arrival) made a strong impression on me; and from that moment, at every step which the two armies advanced towards each other, the expectation of the spectators was heightened, and the interest increased. The silence of their approach was Grecian *. The king's party was defeated; and the order which he maintained in his retreat is inconceivable. In two hours there

* Οι δ' αρ' ισαν σιγη μενεα πνειοντες Αχαιοι.
In solemn silence march'd the valiant Greeks.

was only ten minutes confusion: near the hill where I stood, there was an eminence covered with trees, which commanded the field of battle; each party was desirous of seizing this post, and some squadrons of cavalry came from both sides full gallop, in silence, till the instant of their entering the wood; they then gave loud shouts, and fought with swords and pistols: fresh troops came from each side to their assistance, and all shouted. The vivacity of this moment is inexpressible. As I know nothing of the art military, I cannot give you the particulars of any evolution; but the regularity and the quickness with which the Prussian soldier performs every thing, astonish the military of all other nations.

The

The battle ended, the imagination saw thefe pictures of Taffo:

Pien tutto il campo è di spezzate lance,
Di rotti scudi e di troncato arnese:
Di spade ai petti, alle squarciate pance
Altre confitte, altre par terra stese;
Di corpi altri supini, altri coi volti,
Quasi mordendo il suol, al suol rivolti.

* *Giace il cavallo al suo signore appresso;*
Giace il compagno appo il compagno estinto;
Giace il nemico appo il nemico; e spesso
Sul morto il vivo, il vincitor sul vinto.
Non v'è silenzio, e non v'è grido espresso;
Mà odi un non so che roco, e indistinto,
Fremiti di furor, mormori d' ira,
Gemiti di chi langue, e di chi spira.

XX. 50, 51.

O'erfpread with fhatter'd arms the ground appears,
With broken bucklers, and with fhiver'd fpears.
Here fwords are ftuck in haplefs warriors kill'd,
And ufelefs there are fcatter'd o'er the field.

* It is a tradition among the Italian poets that this stanza cost Taffo ten months.

Here,

Here, on their face, the breathless bodies lie;
There turn their ghastly features to the sky.

Beside his lord the courser press'd the plain;
Beside his slaughter'd friend the friend is slain:
Foe near to foe; and on the vanquish'd spread
The victor lies; the living on the dead!
An undistinguish'd din is heard around,
Mix'd is the murmur, and confus'd the sound:
The threats of anger, and the soldier's cry,
The groans of those that fall, and those that die.

Hook.

The imagination, I say, formed these pictures, and the heart congratulated itself that they were but imaginary.

If I had great curiosity to see two armies engaged, I had much more to see the king. At length he came: he was not so tall as I expected; this circumstance excepted, he answered all the ideas that I had formed of him:

his air and countenance bespoke the king, the hero, and the man of genius. Thinking I could never see enough of him, I kept close to him all the way to Sans-souci. A great crowd followed him; some peasants waited to see him at the entrance of his palace, and cried, 'Long live the 'king!' He pulled off his hat several times to them. This was twice that he deceived me; the first time by his stature, the second by his politeness.

LETTER III.

BERLIN.

THE next day there was another battle: the manœuvres were different; but I did not understand them. Before I went to it I visited the king's king's apartments. You go through the eating-parlour and the concert-room into the bed-chamber. I aſked the Swiſs, " Which was the king's chamber?"—' This.' I expected a magnificent bed. There was a fine alcove at the end of the room, but no bed in it.—" Where is the bed?" —' There.' Behind a little ſkreen, in a corner, was a ſmall bed, very narrow, with curtains of green ſilk; this was his. On the other ſide of the caſtle were ſeveral beds in the ſame taſte, then occupied by his generals. The carpet on which he ſteps when he gets out of bed, is very coarſe. There was another ſmall couch, where ſometimes a page ſleeps when the king is ill, and three or four tables covered with books and papers.

I aſked

I asked my conductor (a Swiss wit, who has lived eighteen years with his majesty) " where was the king's ward-" robe?" He replied, ' on his back *.'

The last time of my seeing him was at Berlin. He came thither to receive the adieus of the Baron de Swieten, minister from their Imperial Majesties, and to give audience to the new minister the Count de Cobenzl †.

[* Dr. Moore has given a list of the king's cloaths; viz. two blue coats, faced with red, the lining of one a little torn; two yellow waistcoats, a good deal soiled with Spanish snuff; three pair of yellow breeches, and a suit of blue velvet, embroidered with silver, for grand occasions.]

† I had not the honour of knowing this gentleman, as I left Berlin two days after his arrival. But his cousin, the Count de Cobenzl, who attended the emperor in his travels, is one of the most amiable and interesting characters in Germany.

the foreign ministers, the persons who were to be presented, and the military, were all that were at court. We were ten English: the king spoke to the first and the last, not on account of their situation, but because their names struck him. The first was major Dalrymple*. To him the king said, "You have been presented "to me before?—I ask your ma"jesty's pardon: it was my uncle." Mr. Pitt was the last. The king, "Are you a relation of lord Chatham?" "Yes, Sire."—"He is a man whom I "highly esteem."

He then went to the foreign ministers, and talked more to prince Dolgoroucki, the Russian ambassador, than

* Author of "Travels through Spain and Portugal in 1774."

to any other. In the midst of his conversation with this prince, he turned abruptly to Mr. Elliot, the English minister, and asked him the name of the duchess of Kingston. This transition was less Pindaric than it appears; he had just been speaking of the court of Petersburg, and that lady was then there.

LETTER IV.

Berlin.

THERE never was a fat soldier seen in any country; but the king of Prussia has not a fat serjeant. A profound knowledge of the œconomy of finance is one of the points in which this prince excells; it is also one

one of the reasons why his troops seldom grow fat. The money which other sovereigns expend on mistresses, pomp, hunting-parties, &c. he employs on things that are necessary, and in rewarding merit. During the time that I was at Berlin, the artillery was exercised for a fortnight: an officer of that corps told me, that there was consumed every day 100 louis d'ors worth of gunpowder. The king is not lavish of his bounties; but his generosity to general Leschwitz, to the widow of colonel Quintus*, and to many other persons of merit, is well

[* A favourite officer whom the king romanised (we cannot say christened) by the name of *Quintus Icilius*, on account of his profound knowledge of the Greek and Roman tactics. His real name was Charles Guischard.]

known.

known. Every officer with whom you converse will give you some fresh instance of the liberality of his master.

I am fond of my subject, and I could write to you a long time of the Great Frederick; but after relating a little anecdote, I will say a word of his poetry, and then we will proceed to Dresden.

Two days after my return from Potsdam, Count ****, a French traveller, who lodged at my hotel, asked my leave to visit me. We talked of the city, of the manœuvres, of the king. At ten o'clock at night he entered my apartment:—' My dear ' friend,' said he, (he had seen me for half an hour that morning) ' I am ' come to take leave of you.'—" Why " so?"—' The king has just requested ' me

' me to quit the town, and I know not
' the reason, unless it be, that when I
' walk the streets, I take the plan of
' any building that strikes me.'—" Has
" the king said any thing particular of
" you?" 'No,' replied he briskly,
' he has said nothing ill of me, but
' he thinks the more; I have sent
' for horses, and I set out in half an
' hour.' "But," said I, "I do not see
" the necessity of your setting out in a
" night like this" (it rained violently);
" you may wait till to-morrow." 'Par-
' don me,' replied he, ' his majesty
' may change his mind, to-morrow
' perhaps he may requeſt me to stay*.'
This foreigner was not known by any
one, not even by his own minister; he

* He was apprehensive of being sent to Span-
daw.

seemed

seemed well educated, and was about forty.

When a poet has a richness of ideas and of expression, every time that we read him we discover new beauties: this is the case with Horace and with the king of Prussia. There is not, most certainly, an author in the French language who has more thoughts, or more vigorous thoughts, than this prince. All his productions spring from a strong and brilliant imagination, always regulated by a solid judgment, which, in my opinion, constitutes the perfection of genius. In all his works the most sage philosophy and the profoundest morality are blended with the most poignant wit and the happiest sallies. When his subjects admit of it, his style

style is no less poignant than emphatical. He has emulated Horace, and he has been able to equal him even in his best pieces; for in many respects the Pindar of the North would be dishonoured by comparing him with the Latin poet. Horace has not a more sincere admirer than myself, but there are many of his works which I cannot read without disgust. One cannot find a single middling composition of the King-Poet; and no enthusiast of Horace will deny that he has many. One cannot find in this prince any mean or indecent passage; Horace abounds with things that are vulgar and offensive. You will answer, that the souls of the Monarch and of Horace were different, their education different, and their

situations

situations in life different; this confirms my assertion. I will not always determine in favour of his versification; but in strength and vivacity of colouring Rubens does not surpass him.

He has written an epistle *on Travelling**, in order to prevent the young Germans from going to ruin themselves at Paris and London; in these three verses he speaks of one of those gentlemen † at his return:

[* Addressed to Count Rottembourg.]
† I cannot help here mentioning a story which I heard at Paris of a young German traveller. He had been told that the Venetian ambassador was to make his entry at court, and that it was a magnificent sight: he flew to Versailles, he arived at the chapel-door, from whence he saw the chancellor *coming out* in a long blue mantle: he asks his neighbour, " Pray, Sir, is that *cardi-*
" *nal in blue* the Venetian ambassador making his
" entry?"

De stupide qu'il fut, il est devenu fât,
Et jouant l'étourdi sans pouvoir jamais l'être,
C'est un lourdaut badin qui fait le petit-maître.

From stupid dolt he grows an errant fool,
Acting, not being, a blunderhead complete,
The waggish dunce at length becomes a fop.

How many originals of more countries than one does this portrait represent!

LETTER V.

BERLIN,

LIGHT and heat are every where diffused through the works of the philosopher of Sans-souci. In two large volumes of his poetry there is not one barren page; and what makes them truly precious is, that every page breathes the love of humanity.

I

I forefee your objections; and I again demand one opinion for war, and another for peace. No man ever knew the human heart better than Shakfpeare; no man ever drew a character better. This is what he puts into the mouth of an amiable hero;

> In peace there's nothing fo becomes a man,
> As gentlenefs and mild humanity;
> But when the blaft of war blows in our ears,
> Let us be tigers in our fierce deportment.
>
> *Henry* V.

You would think that Shakfpeare meant to fpeak of the king of Pruffia.

Read his odes *on War* and *on the Troubles of the North,* and then judge of the poet and the man:

[When

[When will thy frantic rage, with ruthless hand,
Bellona, cease to desolate the land?
Why do we see on every plain and flood
Such torrents lavish'd of heroic blood?
O'er all the earth, with unresisted sway,
 Sword, fire, confusion, plunder, famine, reign,
Nor can the boundless ocean aught survey,
But wrecks of ships destroy'd, and corses of the slain.
Say, does this fiend, with front of brass endued,
Of blood insatiate, though with blood imbrued,
This fiend of war, the world in fetters hold,
Only to range and waste it uncontroul'd?
Old Charon's wherry such enormous weight
 Ne'er yet sustain'd, nor were the fatal sheers
So oft employ'd, of unrelenting Fate,
To snap the vital threads that hold our warriors
 years.
Inhuman Discord, red with carnage, shakes
Her flaming torch, and irritates her snakes,
And, fond of chaos, with eternal strife
Embroils all nature, and imbitters life:
Man's erring steps from gulph to gulph she leads,
 And death, despair, and treason, all the crimes
Which follow and avenge such cruel deeds,
O'erspread with cypress all our desolated climes.]

        What

*What transports seize my soul! what sudden fires!
Some god my senses steals, some god inspires;
'Tis Phœbus' self, his heav'n-born genius deigns
To teach my feeble voice immortal strains.
Let all the world an awful silence keep,
 Ye kings, ye people, listen to my lay,
And let awhile your frantic fury sleep,
To hear the truths I sing, to hear them and obey.
 Ye judges of mankind, their gods by birth,
 Ye proud oppressors of this wretched earth,
 Though by your hands dire thunderbolts are thrown,
 Though in your chains these captive people groan;
Restrain the rigour of resistless force:
 These are your children, feel what fathers feel:
From all their bosoms, stabb'd without remorse,
Streams your own vital flood, and stains the murd'rous steel.
 As a good shepherd, provident and wise,
 Defends his darling flock, with watchful eyes,
 From the wolf's ravenous jaws, with gore imbrued,
 Or the fierce lion, prowling for his food,

[* Mr. Sherlock has quoted only the four following stanzas; but the translator has given the whole ode.]

When

When from the wood the tyrant flies, their
  fears
Remov'd, they foundly sleep or safely feed,
And though his sheep with fondling hand he
  shears,
Yet ne'er beneath his knife the harmless victims
  bleed.

A tender monarch, like this shepherd swain,
Humane in counsels, in designs humane,
For public good alone prolongs his days,
And counts his years by deeds deserving praise:
Wreaths stain'd with blood he nobly scorns to
  wear;
But to his virtues future glory owes:
Such was that ancient, that heroic pair,
Aurelius, Titus thus to deathless honours rose.

[Abhorr'd be these intestine wars, these brands
So widely scatter'd by Ambition's hands:
See! all the universe in ruins lies;
Earth is a tomb of vast stupendous size:
What tragic scenes this theatre disgrace!
Europe against her sons, with step-dame hate,
Leads forth astonish'd Asia's powerful race,
To urge with speedier course the direful work of
  fate.

Barbarians

[31]

Barbarians swarming from Siberia's coasts,
Assassins nurs'd amidst eternal frosts,
Caspians and Tartars, join'd in dread array,
I see, retain'd in Dutch and German * pay:
This savage rage what Dæmon can inspire!
Europe, no more your fury can sustain,
With fierce dissension other worlds to fire,
A lust for fighting fields transports you o'er the main.

From your bright mansion in yon azure sky,
Goddess on whom for bliss we all rely,
So long desir'd, descend, O lovely Peace!
Close Janus' dreadful gates, bid Discord cease;
All interest, envy, banish; and restore
To worth, to arts, that fame, that life they want;
Then we, amidst our laurels stain'd with gore,
Thy myrtles and thy olives joyfully will plant.

His *Art of War* is his master-piece, and the longest of his works. You will there find the most lively images,

[* The author might with much more reason have *said British!* This seems to fix the date of the ode to the year 1748, when the Russians were marching to Flanders, which hastened the peace.]

the

the boldeſt and moſt judicious metaphors, a pencil always manly, always majeſtic, and an impetuoſity in the ſtyle which is irrefiſtible.

When one thinks of all the proofs which this prince has given, in war and in politics, of the fertility of his imagination, and of the ſolidity of his judgment; when one remembers that he has always fed his mind with the moſt perfect productions of the ancient philoſophers and poets; and when we know that he has added to this whatever could be found in the ſociety of the moſt enlightened men and the firſt wits of his age; we ſhall no longer be aſtoniſhed at the variety of merit that is found in his compoſitions. Accept, great king, theſe juſt encomiums; I ſhould not have ſo highly
applauded

applauded your talents, if I were not fully perſuaded of the goodneſs of your heart.

*Reçois l'eloge pur, l'hommage merité;
Je le dois à ton nom, comme à la verité.*
                              Art de la Guerre.

Receive this pure applauſe, this homage due
To your great name, becauſe I know 'tis true.

Read his *Epiſtle to his Siſter of Bareith, on her Illneſs,* and ſee whether every verſe does not flow from a tender and feeling heart.

It will be ſaid that there are faults in his poetry; I leave them for the Zoiluſes to point out; and I ſhall cloſe my letter with his addreſs to young ſoldiers at the concluſion of his *Art of War.*

D

Si votre cœur aspire à la sublime gloire,
Sachez vaincre, et sur-tout user de la victoire.
Le plus grand des Romains, par ses succès * divers,*
Le jour qu'à son pouvoir il soumit l'univers,
Sauva ses ennemis dans les champs de Pharsale.

Voyez à Fontenoy, Louis dont l'ame égale,
Douce dans ses succès, soulage les vaincus,
C'est un Dieu bienfaisant dont ils sont secourus;
Ils baisent en pleurant la main qui les désarme,
Sa valeur les soumet, sa clémence les charme,
Dans le sein des fureurs la bonté trouve lieu,
Si vaincre est d'un Heros, pardonner est d'un Dieu.

To heights of glory if your heart aspires,
Know how to conquer, and your conquest use:
The greatest, most succesful † Roman chief,
On that fam'd day when he subdu'd the world,
Sav'd ev'n his foes in dire Pharsalia's field.

    Lewis with equal mind at Fontenoy,
Mild in succefs, his vanquish'd foes consoles;
Like a good deity his aid he gives:
With tears they bathe the hand that has dis-
    arm'd them;
His valour conquers, and his mercy charms:
With goodnefs war's dire horrors he allays;
Heroes may vanquish, but 'tis God forgives.

* Comme politique, ecrivain, et conquérant.
† As a politician, a writer, and a conqueror.

LETTER

THE country of Saxony is very beautiful, the city of Drefden very pretty, and the court one of the moft amiable in Germany; ftrangers no where receive greater civilities: the women are mild, lively, and witty; the climate is fine; the environs pleafant; the fare delicious: it is indeed a charming country, and the Saxons would be too happy if they had not a hero for their neighbour. Ah! dreadful is the neighbourhood of a hero or a volcano! The fituation of Drefden refembles that of Portici; and the inhabitants tremble at a menace of Frederick, like thofe of Portici at a rumbling of Vefuvius. An old

old woman spoke to me of the bombardment of the city in the last war, with the same horror* of recollection, and almost in the same terms, as an old man at Portici spoke to me of the terrible eruption in 1768.

Nothing gives so perfect an image of war as the lava. Imagine a rich country covered with vines, pastures, and corn: bursts forth a torrent of fire, and in an instant the most brilliant landscape is changed into the most dismal picture that nature can present. This is the history of an eruption of Vesuvius: it is that of the Palatinate set on fire by Turenne.

Travellers in general make too short a stay at Dresden, and they are in the wrong. It is a country highly

* *Mens meminisse horret.*

interesting

interesting to all who are fond of natural history, pictures, and the beauties of nature of every kind. If the Pruffians are the Macedonians of Germany, the Saxons are its Athenians. I have scarcely seen a country where there is more taste, or more chearful and agreeable society.

It is at the Vatican that we learn to admire the master-pieces of Raphael; it is at Dresden that we learn to value the pictures of Corregio. Raphael is almost universally acknowledged as the monarch of the picturesque kingdom. A consular government would please me better; I would wish him to have Corregio for his colleague. I know that I shall have all the demi-connoisseurs against me, and I will tell them the reason; either they have

have not seen the most beautiful paintings of this master, or they have seen them superficially. His best works are at Parma and Dresden, and these are two cities that the traveller sees post. He passes three mornings perhaps in this gallery; he wishes to see every thing, and consequently sees nothing. It is the same repetition at Parma; and then he arrives at Rome. In all the companies where he goes, when painting is the subject, he hears no one named but Raphael. If a foreigner mentions Corregio, the Romans say, that he has great merit; but they do not feel what they say; for they have only seen some indifferent pictures of his that are at Rome: these pictures they compare with the master-pieces of Raphael;

and

and you may guess their inference.
The truth is, that they esteem Corregio as many modern philosophers
adore Newton, by hear-say. To determine right, the *Night* * should be
placed beside the *Transfiguration*; the
Magdalen †, or the *Venus* ‡, by the
Galatea; the *St. Jerom*, the *St. George*,

[* The famous *Notte di Corregio*, a nativity, is in the duke's palace at Modena: It is so far a night-piece as that all the light of the picture flows from the infant, who seems perfectly to shine. . . . This thought has been followed by great numbers of others. *Wright*.

The late general Guise, equally famous for his oaths and his connoisseurship, used to swear that this picture alone would illuminate a dark room.]

[† This is also at Modena. It is a Magdalen lying alone and reading, with her head raised up and supported by her right hand. It is most highly finished, but rather over laboured. This famous picture is closeted up, and when shewn is brought forth with great solemnity. *Wright*.]

[‡ An inestimable picture in the possession of Sir William Hamilton.]

or the *St. Sebastian*, beside the *School of Athens*, and the other pictures of the Vatican.

The Romans are not good judges of painting; they determine well of certain parts. In every thing relating to composition and design their judgment is sure; and in those two points Raphael has no equal. As to colouring they know little of it: accustomed to consider Raphael as a perfect model, they think his colouring also perfect; but the falshood of this idea is too notorious for me to mention it. I do not pretend to talk of painting like an artist; but I have studied pictures much, and I shall always think that one of the first objects of painting is to deceive the eye, and to make the spectator

believe

believe that the figures which are on the canvafs are not there; in this part of the art Corregio is unrivalled. The magic of his pencil abfolutely detaches his figures from the cloth; and, with this relief, they have a foftnefs * to which no painter has ever approached. Nothing can be farther from my thoughts than to detract from the merit of Raphael; it is too well eftablifhed; and if I could prove that he had none, I do not fee that this would add to the reputation of Corregio. All that I afk is to be allowed that there are two fine eyes and two fine eyes; which travellers will not allow, for the reafon that I have mentioned,

* *Moëlleux* in French; *morbidazza* in Italian.

their

their having formed their taste at Rome, where Corregio is not known.

We shall have another reason for extolling Corregio, when we compare his situation with that of Raphael. Poor and unconnected, he lived in a small town, where he had no master but his genius, no model but nature, no attendants but the Graces, and the necessity of procuring bread for his family, to incite him. Behold Raphael at Rome, patronized by the sovereign, courted (in consequence) by princes and cardinals, hoping to become a cardinal himself, surrounded by the works of the Greeks, and by great artists his rivals, who, by their criticisms, at once stimulated and improved him. What advantages over the poor and amiable

amiable Corregio! who was obliged to go on foot to Parma, carrying on his back thofe *chef d'oeuvres* of which one at prefent makes the riches of a cabinet.

No painter ever defigned like Raphael; no painter knew the *clair-obfcur* fo well as Corregio: Raphael is always correct and noble; Corregio has often negligences: Raphael took many ideas from the ancient ftatues and bas-reliefs; Corregio pillaged only nature: Raphael has all the majeftic, Corregio all the amiable, graces. The queftion cannot be decided; Raphael is Juno with the girdle of Venus; Corregio is Venus herfelf.

There is a faying of this painter which has always pleafed me: The Bolognefe had defired Raphael to paint them

them a picture; he gave them the celebrated St. Cecilia *. The fame of this work brought Corregio to Bologna to see it; after gazing on it for half an hour in a profound silence, he said, ' *And I too am a painter.*' Yes, enchanting artist, you might well say so; and while men trust their eyes and feelings, many will be of your opinion. This exclamation is admirable, it shews me the man. It is a superior genius who sees without jealousy the master-piece of a contemporary, who dares to do him justice, and who, at the same time, sensible of his own merit, exclaims with a noble and modest simplicity, ' And I have also talents!'

[* This picture is in the church of St. *Giovanni in Monte*. The Saint, enraptured with the harmony of a choir of angels, dashes all her musical instruments against the ground. *Keysler.*]

'This

This struck Montesquieu in the same manner: "When I have seen [*], says he, what so many great men in France, in England, and in Germany, have writ before me, I have been in admiration, but I have not lost my courage; *and I too am a painter* [†]," exclaimed I with Corregio."

LETTER VII.

Vienna, *March* 3, 1778.

HOW rich is the universe in delights! How many pleasures may a virtuous and prudent man enjoy in his travels! If his view be to seek for amiable and enlightened cha-

[*] Preface to the *Spirit of Laws*.
[†] *Ed anch' Io son pittore.*

racters, he will find them every where; and if he knows how to value them, they will receive him well. Vienna has its beautiful fides; the national character is good, and thofe whofe education is the leaft cultivated may there be fafely trufted. Its air is healthy, fharp, dry, and very cold. The ideas which moft ftrike foreigners are the affability of the court, the magnificence of the entertainments, and the beauty of the fair fex. Three days after my arrival I was at a ball, where there were thirty young ladies, all handfome. They drefs with tafte, and dance well. The beft dancer was the countefs Dirheim. She is a canonefs, and the moft beautiful canonefs that ever was. Of all the perfons I have ever feen, fhe is at
firft

first sight the most striking. A painter could find only one fault in her, and that fault is a small one. If I were a poet, I would here draw her picture; but Ariosto has done it; it is his Alcina:

> *Di persona era tanto ben formata,*
> *Quanto mè' finger san pittori industri, &c.*

> - A shape whose like in wax 'twere hard to frame,
>   Or to express by skill of painters rare, &c.

You never saw so pretty a mouth; this stanza seems made on purpose to paint it:

> *Sotto quel sta, quasi fra due vallette,*
> *La bocca sparsa di natio cinabro;*
> *Quive due filze son di perle elette,*
> *Che chiude ed apre une bello de dolce labro;*
> *Quindi escon le cortesi parolette*
> *Da render molle ogni cor rozzo e scabro;*
> *Quivi si forma quel soave riso,*
> *Ch' apre a sua posta in terra il Paradiso.*

vii. 13.

Conjoin'd

Conjoin'd to which in due and comely space,
Doth stand the mouth stain'd with vermillion
  hue,
Two rows of precious pearl serve, in their place,
To shew and shut a lip right fair to view:
Hence come the courteous words, and full of grace,
That mollify hard hearts, and make them new;
From hence proceed those smilings sweet and nice,
That seem to make an earthly Paradise.
Harrington.

The Princess Charles Lichtenstein, the Countess Paar, and the Princess Lignoski, are the three prettiest women in Germany; the Countess Wurmbrand, and the Countess Buquoy, at Vienna, and the Countess Loss at Dresden, are the three finest German women I have seen. Perhaps there is a more beautiful head than that of the Countess of Wurmbrand in Paradise, but on earth there certainly is not.

As

As to wit, the Countefs Bergen has unqueftionably the moft; the Countefs Degenfield, wife of the Dutch envoy, is highly accomplifhed and amiable; and the Baronefs of Rheifhach has as much real merit as I have feen in my travels, a great deal of wit, an improved underftanding, and a good heart; fhe is a charming woman in every fenfe of the word.

You will fee in Prince Kaunitz a fuperior genius, and one of the greateft men of the age. He gives a moft gracious reception to the Englifh, and has fome of them every day at his table. His houfe is open every evening, and there you will always find part of the diplomatic body, which is here very numerous and refpectable. Monfeigneur Gerampi, the

E   Pope's

Pope's Nuncio, is full of good-nature and erudition. He is much beloved at Vienna and at Rome, and with reason. There is not an Englishman, or any man who speaks truth, who passes through Vienna, without doing justice to Sir Robert Keith. He is indisputably one of the first geniuses in Europe: his soul and his understanding appear in his eye; it is a clear, quick, penetrating, firm eye. Few men possess like him the secret of pleasing every one.

The houshold of the Baron de Breteuil is royally established. We were five and twenty English, and this ambassador invited us all every week of the Carnaval to a ball and a supper. There were always more than 200 persons, excellent cheer, French wines,

wines, Tokay, &c. &c. There is no house here more agreeable than his. No idea, I confess, has given me more offence, in many young travellers of different nations whom I have met, than that of not doing justice to persons of distinguished merit. This mode of acting appears to me base and unworthy of a man well born, even if those persons were unknown to us; but it is the height of ingratitude to speak ill of those who have shewn us civilities, to disown their favours, or even to be silent when an occasion offers of speaking of them.

Vienna is perhaps the best city in Europe to teach a young traveller the manners of the great world: at his arrival he will be introduced into all the beſt houſes; and if he is an Engliſhman, he will meet with the moſt flattering reception, becauſe Sir Robert Keith, who is univerſally eſteemed, accompanies him every where; but every foreigner is well received, eſpecially by the ladies, who are very well bred, and extremely amiable.

You will afterwards be entertained according to your deſert; if you are ſimple in your manners, and noble in all your proceedings, you will be enchanted with Vienna; and if, when you leave the country, you do not make its elogium, you will be your own ſatiriſt.

LETTER

LETTER VIII.

Vienna.

THERE are here a German theatre and an Italian one, both bad. There is only one woman* who has merit. Though she has neither beauty nor air, she plays with such judgment, and has such expression in her looks, her actions, and her cadence, that she even interests those who are unacquainted with the language.

You will here see some singular sights; the procession of the knights of the golden fleece is superb; the Hungarian guards, who come to court on New-year's-day, are the most brilliant troop in Europe; but the most

* *La Sacco.*

striking

ſtriking ſight, and which is really beautiful, is the courſe of *traineaux*. The Archdutcheſs of Milan, the Archdutcheſs Mary-Elizabeth, and the Princeſs Schwarzenberg, were conducted by the Archduke of Milan, the Archduke Maximilian, and Prince Albert of Saxony: they were followed by twenty-five ladies, all in crimſon velvet with a very broad gold lace; the dreſſes of the knights were of a ſky-blue velvet, laced like thoſe of the ladies. There were ſome equipages that coſt a thouſand guineas. On each ſide of the horſe were two running-foot-men, dreſſed with an elegance ſuitable to the equipage.

This is one of the happy moments in the life of a Vienneſe lady; it is the moment in which ſhe makes the

moſt

most pompous display of her riches and of her charms. Embellished with all her graces, her head studded with diamonds, her bosom uncovered, she seems a Venus in her car; and knowing that she is the object of the admiration of some thousands of persons, she shews the satisfaction of her heart by a perpetual smile. In every country the fair go dressed to public places to be seen *: but here the women make the show; and the pleasure with which this idea inspires them is so lively, that it makes them entirely forget the rigours of the season. It is not so with the poor knight; having no enjoyment, but that of admiring his fair-one's *chignon*, he perishes with cold: in fact men have

* *Spectatum* [ornatæ] *veniunt, spectentur ut ipsæ.*

been frequently obliged to retire before the expiration of thefe two hours, on account of the feverity of the cold; but no woman was ever known to complain of it.

The courfe begins in the great fquare before the Imperial palace; they take feveral turns there, and after traverfing the principal ftreets of the city, they return thither to finifh it. The ground of fnow, on which this moving picture winds, relieves its fplendor extremely, and makes the fight the richeft and moft dazzling that can be conceived.

But the fight that gives a foreigner the moft pleafure at Vienna, is that which he fees in the anti-chamber of prince Kaunitz, once a week, after dinner: it is a concourfe of all the

indigent

indigent who are in need of protection, and who come thither assured of finding it: the ear of this prince is never shut to the complaints of the poor, and his hand is always ready to give them assistance.

LETTER IX.

VIENNA.

YOU should not leave Vienna without seeing Metastasio: he is a lively old man and an agreeable companion. He is the greatest poet that Italy has produced since Tasso: I would have said the greatest that she has ever had, were he not a living author; on which account he must not be praised too much. Read his

his *Canzonettes*, in particular that which begins *Grazie agl' inganni tuoi**, and say, what Italian poet has written with so much purity, so much elegance, and so much grace? He embellishes whatever he touches, and appears to me absolutely the first that has established true principles of good taste in Italy. In those little compositions there is a native beauty and freshness in the colouring, a simplicity and delicacy in the thoughts and sentiments, that makes them enchanting.

Metastasio is not wanting in any one of the requisites that constitute a great poet. Born with sensibility,

[* *The Indifferent*. See three good translations of this Ode, in the second volume of Dodsley's Collection, by Richard Roderick, esq. the Rev. Mr. Seward, and an unknown hand. A fourth, with still more spirit and closeness, by Isaac Pacatus Shard, esq. is in the sixth volume of Nichols's Collection.]

with

with a profound and penetrating understanding, and with a lively and fertile imagination, he poffeffed all that he could derive from nature: at twelve years of age he went into the family of the celebrated Gravina: that learned critic, who faw the *tinfel*, the *glittering extravagances*, and the *barren abundance* of the Italian writers, fhewed Metaftafio that the true fource of a fure tafte was the Greek authors. The young pupil adopted this idea, examined the principles of thofe poets, and on their principles he has written all his life. Italy is little calculated at prefent to infpire fublime fentiments; it gives a perfect knowledge of the tender paffions: in Italy he paffed his youth; there he learned to write his *Demetrio*,

his

his *Olympiade*, and his *Demofoonte*. At the age of twenty-five he went into Germany; his residence at Vienna, and the reading of Corneille, elevated his mind; he wrote his *Regulo*, and his *Clemenza di Tito*. No author has better understood Horace; few poets have so well executed his ideas:

Scribendi recte sapere est et principium et fons.
Sound judgment is the ground of writing well:
Roscommon.

He studied philosophy; and he did not begin to treat of a subject till he had thoroughly examined it.

Omne supervacuum pleno de pectore manat,
All superfluities are soon forgot,
Roscommon.

is an observation, of which he felt the wisdom; and he has written with as much rapidity as precision.

He

He felt the value of Boileau as well as of Horace; and he has never fwerved from thofe great principles.

Tout doit tendre au bon-fens;
Rien n'eft beau que le vrai, le vrai feul eft aimable.
Let fenfe be ever in your view;
Nothing is beautiful that is not true;
The true alone is lovely.

The perfons who have compofed mufic for his verfes, and thofe who fing and repeat them, are beft able to judge of the harmony of his poetry: in thefe two claffes there is but one opinion from Peterfburg to Naples.

No Italian has fo well developed the emotions of the foul, nor fucceeded equally in moving and interefting his reader. Metaftafio rofe to the fublime; but he was born tender, and one may fay, without wronging any

any nation, that few of their poets have so well painted the tender passions, or made such lively impressions on the heart.

When one examines his works well, and compares them with the Gothic productions of Dante, with the absurdities of Ariosto, with the extravagances of Marini, and with the puerilities of Tasso, one is astonished at the decision of the Italians: they prefer Tasso to Metastasio, and Ariosto to Tasso; but there is no disputing with the Italians upon poetry; they deny all the principles admitted in every other country.

I am far from speaking here against the talents of the Italians; they have perhaps more than any other nation in Europe; but these talents are uncultivated,

cultivated, and of many reasons the most essential is, that there are no Mæcenases.

I hope you do not imagine that I deny that Dante had an astonishing genius, and that he has some passages of the highest sublime; that the genius of Ariosto was easy and fertile; that no one tells a story better; that he has some descriptions exquisitely beautiful; and that his *Orlando Furioso* is a poem full of gaiety and variety. Marini had a vast imagination; but he is madder than Ariosto.

I am only the friend of truth; and if I do not deny the merit of these poets, much less shall I deny that of Tasso. Nature perhaps was less generous to him than to them; but his poems would be placed above theirs

at

at Paris, at London, and at Athens. That the *Jerufalem Delivered* has many defects, that it has falfe thoughts, fome playing upon words, and much tinfel, is certain; but it is alfo certain that it has much gold. The fubject is moſt happy; the conduct of the poem in general is fage; its march, majeſtic; its language, noble and well fupported, and its verſification always beautiful: it has the pathetic, and it has the fublime. The *Aminta* is a maſter-piece of elegance and ſimplicity, and is much more perfect than the *Gerufalemme Liberata*.

Metaftafio feems to me to have more natural talents than Taffo, all his beauties, and many more, and none of his faults. He fatisfies the underſtanding, he delights the ear,

he

he enchants the imagination, he captivates the heart; and for thefe reafons he will always be the poet of men of fenfe, the poet of women, and the poet of all perfons who have tafte.

LETTER X.

The Hague, June 10, 1777.

THE face of the country in Holland is fingular, and very ftriking for three days: after that time, one fees nothing but the fame flat repetition of fields always level, interfected by canals which are all alike; and on thofe canals barks all made on the fame model. Every traveller fhould pafs through Holland, as the ideas which it gives are found no where elfe, and

[66]

he will soon collect them. Throughout Holland the four elements are bad; the cardinal virtue of the country is cleanliness; the deities adored, Mercury and Plutus; but as for Apollo and the Nine Sisters, one never hears them named.

Their school of painting deserves to be viewed, in order to have an idea of the height to which the mechanism of the art may be carried. Their finish is much more perfect than that of the Italians; but as they only servilely copy an ungrateful nature, one of their pictures never makes us wish to see it again. Their absolute want of taste makes them despise all that belongs to the Italian school; the antique is with them a term of ridicule; and if an artist were to work

there

there, on these ideas, he would die of hunger. In a cabinet at Amsterdam I recollected what Lewis XIV. said of a picture of a Dutch feast, full of all those disgusting ideas which accompany a drunken debauch, '*Take away those baboons.*' This expression is worthy of the age of Boileau, Moliere, and Racine, in which the imitations of beautiful and noble nature alone could please. This picture was by one of the first masters, and perfectly well painted; but if the nature that is chosen be disgusting, the more perfect the imitation is, the more offensive is the picture; and those who can admire such productions have a mean and depraved taste.

The taste of the age of Lewis XIV. no longer exists in France: The Dutch pictures

pictures are those which are most in fashion; and they sell at Paris at incredible prices. It is shameful for the French, who are actually delicate, and who have such collections as those of Versailles, the Luxembourg, and the *Palais Royal*, to suffer themselves to be led away by a mode the most disgraceful for them that they have ever adopted. but ju...r...d to Rubens, to whom nature by mistake gave birth in their neighbourhood, is not relished by the Dutch; and the proof of it is, no young painter imitates him. If they value his pictures, it is because they sell well; and if some of his pictures still remain among them, it is because travellers will not give six times more for them than they are worth.

There

There is one object only in this country with which you will be much pleased; that is, Sir Joseph Yorke: the King of England is well represented in all the courts that I have seen; but certainly he has no representative that does him more honour than this ambassador. His merit alone forces from me this elogium; for he shewed only common civilities to a man without a title, modest to an extreme, and who has little other merit than that of being highly sensible of the merit of others.

All great men have many persons who are envious of them; Sir Joseph Yorke ought to have more than any one else; but his is the *only* character in Europe against which I have not heard a single word. Dignity and
good-

many courts as cardinals; every cardinal is a kind of prince, and may become a sovereign; this reason alone may convince you that this country must have more hypocritical characters than any other.

Of all the sovereigns whom I have seen, the pope represents majesty the best; the cardinals are like Martial's epigrams; there are some good, some bad, and many indifferent. Almost all of them derive honour from their rank; the cardinal de Bernis is an exception, he does honour to the purple by his virtues and his talents.

The women are reserved in public, and in private extravagant to a degree; the prelates, effeminate; the nobility,

nobility *, illiterate; and the people, wicked.

The studies generally pursued are, the laws, antiquities, and divinity, because these are the three principal roads that here lead to fortune. A poet is considered as a † dangerous, or at best as an useless being; and for this reason a poetical talent is rather oppressed than encouraged. Metastasio could not there fine bread.

You will often have occasion to admire the genius of Corneille for the truth with which he has drawn the Roman women. The assurance of their eye, the firmness of their step, every feature of their face, and every movement of their body, de-

* The Duke of Ceri, the Marquis of Maccarani, and two or three more, are exceptions.
† *Fœnum habet in cornu, aiunt.*

many courts as cardinals; every cardinal is a kind of prince, and may become a sovereign; this reason alone may convince you that this country must have more hypocritical characters than any other.

Of all the sovereigns whom I have seen, the pope represents majesty the best; the cardinals are like Martial's epigrams; there are some good, some bad, and many indifferent. Almost all of them derive honour from their rank; the cardinal de Bernis is an exception, he does honour to the purple by his virtues and his talents.

The women are reserved in public, and in private extravagant to a degree; the prelates, effeminate; the nobility,

nobility *, illiterate; and the people, wicked.

"The studies generally pursued are, the laws, antiquities, and divinity, because these are the three principal roads that here lead to fortune. A poet is considered as a † dangerous, or at best as an useless being; and for this reason a poetical talent is rather oppressed than encouraged. Metastasio could not there find bread.

You will often have occasion to admire the genius of Corneille for the truth with which he has drawn the Roman women. The assurance of their eye, the firmness of their step, every feature of their face, and every movement of their body, de-

* The Duke of Ceri, the Marquis of Maccarani, and two or three more, are exceptions.
† *Fænum habet in cornu, aiunt.*

clare

clare the boldness of their souls. They have a very noble air, which is heightened by trailing robes, which they all wear, down to the women of the third degree.

The nation has something like pride, which does not displease me; it is that sort of haughtiness you see in a man of an ancient family fallen to decay. But it has a desire of disguising itself, which pleases no one. The first proverb of the country is, * *He who knows not how to dissemble, knows not how to live*; and they all know how to live. They love obscurity in every thing; and though this idea may seem to you trifling, it is not so: Rome is the worst lighted city in Europe; the

* *Chi non sa fingere, non sa vivere.*

servants

servants do not carry flambeaux; and the first princes of the country, in other respects extremely luxurious, only carry a small dark lanthorn behind their coaches.

The Roman has naturally depth of understanding and strength of character; he is easily moved; and when he is moved, he is violent to an excess. If the dress of the country were military, as you walk the streets you would think yourself in ancient Rome; the faces that you meet so much resemble the characters that history has transmitted to us. This idea has often struck me among the men, and it is still more striking in the women. You will often say, ' There is a woman who might well ' be the mother of a Gracchus, and
' there

"there is another who might produce
"a Sylla!" The number of Messalinas
is small, that of Lucretias less, and
for Sempronias you will find them
rather at Naples than at Rome.

The following is a mark of national
distinction between a Roman and a
Neapolitan woman: a woman of Naples is less modest than one of Rome,
and more bashful; Neapolitan women
have been often seen to blush, but it
is not possible to put a Roman woman
out of countenance.

This is a slight sketch of the present state of that

*Rome, dont le destin dans la paix, dans la guerre,
Est d'être en tous les temps maîtresse de la terre;*
Rome, ever doom'd by fate in peace, in war,
To be the mistress of the world;

* *Qui sæpius petunt vires, quam petuntur,*

And

[77]

And where at present

*Des prêtres fortunés foulent d'un pied tranquille
Les tombeaux des Catons et la cendre d'Emile:*

Priests, happy priests, with tranquil footsteps tread
On tombs and ashes of the mighty dead.

But in my sketch I may easily be mistaken; for of all the countries that I have seen, this is the most difficult to know.

———

LETTER XII.

Rome.

THE point of view from whence is seen the most perfect union of the sublime and beautiful in nature, is from the top of Vesuvius. The point of view from whence is seen the most perfect union of the sub-

lime

[78]

lime and beautiful in art, is in the court of the Apollo of Belvedere. From the former one sees the mouth of the volcano, fields desolated by rivers of lava now frozen, a country of vineyards of considerable extent diversified by the most beautiful mixture of plains and hills, the city of Naples, the hill of Posilipo, a number of islands scattered in a vast sea, &c. &c. &c.

In the court one sees the Apollo, the Laocoon, the Antinöus, and the celebrated *Torso* of Hercules *, which is called "the Torso of Michael Angelo," on account of the admiration which he had for this precious frag-

[* A mutilated antique statue, of which there are now left only the body and thighs.
Wright.]

ment.

ment. Here we see what the Greek nation was. Let me not be told of prejudice for the ancients; I have none; I only do justice to the merit of things, and it is very indifferent to me where they are found, or who are their authors. To be just, one must sometimes appear extravagant: when an object is transcendently beautiful or great, suitable encomiums ought to be given to it. The pen of man cannot do justice to the poetry of Shakspeare, to the genius of the King of Prussia, or to the works of the Greeks. Many, I know, will condemn me for this last expression; I refuse them all as judges; they will condemn me only because they do not know my subjects.

It

It is there, I say, in the Belvedere, that one sees the superiority of the Greeks to all the nations of the world. The distance that is between the Apollo, the Laocoon, and all the best works of the French and the Italians, is so great, that it is almost ridiculous to name them together.

Let the young traveller, when he views the Apollo, recollect that what he sees has been a rude block of marble. The first step for the artist was to create the character of this god. Before, therefore, the marble was touched, the sculptor had made an effort of genius, and that effort of genius was so great, that all the men who have succeeded him to this moment, have never been able to make one like it. This elogium, you say,

say, is too strong; it is not an elogium; it is a fact that I mention: if the fact be not true, name me a statue equal in invention. Is it the * Susanna of Fiammingo, the Justice of Gulielmo della Porta, the Santa Bibiena of Bernini †, or is it the Moses ‡ of Michael Angelo? I do not believe that any man of sense will ever compare them. The Moses is not inferior to any Italian or French statue; but if one had not seen the Torso, from which it is evident that Michael Angelo took the original idea of his statue, one

[* This statue by Du Quesnoy, surnamed il Fiammingo, or the Fleming, is in the church of S. Maria di Loretto.]
[† The master-piece of that sculptor, on the high altar of the church of St. Bibiena at Rome. *Keysler.*]
[‡ In the monument of Julius II. a statue more than twice as big as the life. *Wright.*]

would never be astonished at the invention of that production. The invention of the Apollo astonishes all men, and astonishes them in proportion to the time and attention with which they examine it.

The Apollo of Bernini, notwithstanding its faults, is a fine statue; it appears indifferent only because we compare it (often imperceptibly) with the Apollo of Belvedere. Neither is the Apollo of Bouchardon by any means an indifferent production; but compare the original French statue with the copy of the Greek statue in the gardens of Versailles, the difference is incredible; it is the difference that there is between a man and a god. We cannot tell what a heathen deity was; but we always feel, on viewing

this

this ftatue, that it is the image of fomething more than human.

When genius is unaccompanied by tafte, it is often furprifed at miffing its effect; the character created, it remained for tafte to chufe a moment to fhew this divinity; that moment ought to be animating and interefting; it ought to be favourable to grace, majefty, and expreffion; and it ought to be fo chofen, that the difpofition of the whole, and the diftribution of each part of the ftatue, fhould feem to flow from it with fimplicity and eafe. The artift then has chofen the inftant in which this god gives the fublimeft proof of his divinity by an action of benevolence, in deftroying an enemy of mankind: it is the inftant after he has fhot his arrow at the serpent Python; the arrow discharged, he follows it with his eyes to observe its effect; the expression of each part of the body corresponds to that of the face; and from an idea so simple, this Grecian has been able to form a work which has obtained the applauses of all men, and has made every artist despair.

When a perfect execution is added to genius and taste, man, I think, cannot go farther. The finish of this Apollo is inconceivable, even to the most minute particulars, but the artist might almost have been excused the trouble of so perfectly completing his work; his conception is so sublime, and his distribution so happy, that they alone would have commanded the admiration of all men of all countries;

countries; and a proof of this is the homage every where paid to the cafts of this breathing god.

The beft way to give you an idea of the fuperiority of the Greek execution, is to cite you a fact. The Laocoon was found with only one arm; they wifhed to have another; feveral artifts attempted it, and all failed: Michael Angelo, the boldeft genius that Italy has had, who conceived the idea of placing the Pantheon in the air, and who made the dome of St. Peter's on the fame dimenfions *, thought that he could

[* That celebrated artift, upon hearing fome perfons extol the Rotonda as a work of antiquity never to be paralleled, faid, that he would not only build a dome equally large, but build it in the air; and he made his affertion good.

Keyfler.]

fucceed

succeed in it; and after having worked at it for two years, abashed and despairing, he broke his work to pieces. Guglielmo della Porta, whose superb mausoleum in St. Peter's shews that he was an artist of the first rank, said, that 'it was impossible to make 'it in marble, but that he would 'make it in clay;' and he made the right arm in clay, as we see it at present; an incontestable proof of the unattainable perfection of the Greek execution.

I allow it to be a bad proof of our being in the right, that a celebrated man is of our opinion; but I think that every reasonable being should well examine before he determines against a judgment so solid as that of Poussin, and a genius so bright

as

as that of Montesquieu: the former studied incessantly the best works ancient and modern, on which this was his decision: '*Raphael compared with the moderns is an angel; compared with the ancients he is an ass.*' Compare the most beautiful figure of Raphael, detached, with the Apollo, and his finest group with the Laocoon, and judge for yourself.

France has no man who does her more honour in foreign countries, or who will do her more with posterity, than Montesquieu: it is well known that he made some stay in Italy, and that he did not view objects like a superficial observer: this was his idea with regard to the Greeks; "*Taste and the arts have been carried by them to such a height, that to think to surpass*

" *surpass them will be always not to*
" *know them.*"

LETTER XIII.

Between ROME *and* NAPLES.

'O HUMAN life!' exclaimed I with Gil Blas, 'how doſt thou abound with misfortunes!' Yes, he is loſt, I ſhall never ſee him more, and my loſs will not afflict him leſs than his afflicts me. At the moment of ſetting out, one has a thouſand things to do; and for fear that my dog ſhould be ſtolen, an hour before my departure I put him into a cloſet, and there I forgot him.

There is no country which gives riſe to ſo many ideas as Rome, and at leaving it I thought of all its beauties ancient and modern; I thought of the poets, I thought of my * book; I often looked at the city; and I considered whether the † expression of Jugurtha was as true at present as when he used it. When my spirits were fatigued, I was going to divert myself with the conversation of my faithful companion—Ah! Heavens! I have forgot him!—I bitterly reproached myself for my giddiness and my ingratitude; I discovered a hundred methods which would have prevented my losing him; I thought of the wisdom of that expression of La Fontaine, ' *Too much of nothing;*' I lost him by too much care.

* Not this, another; [*Consiglio ad un giovane Poeta.*]
† *Urbem venalem cito perituram, si modo emptorem invenerit.*

During

During the remainder of my journey I thought no more of Rome; I forgot *even* my book, I forgot glory, I forgot immortality, and I thought only of my dog. All his good qualities returned to my mind; he was gentle, sprightly, loving; his caresses were sincere, and he bestowed them only on me: he had in my eyes a still farther merit, that of resembling me, he was ugly: this circumstance gave me some hope; ' No,' said I, ' there are few capable of distinguish- ' ing true merit; my dog will be ' found to have ugly ears, and he ' will be restored to me.'

This idea gave me some consolation; and I wrote to my host at Rome to send him to me.

LETTER

LETTER XIV.

NAPLES, *February* 3, 1779.

IT is not surprising that Virgil should make such fine verses at Naples: the air there is so soft and so pure, the sun so brilliant and so warm, and the face of nature so rich and so diversified, that the imagination feels a vivacity and vigour which it scarce ever perceives in other countries.

I am not a poet, but I am very fond of verses, and I have never read them with more pleasure than here. Every time that I go to my window, I feel myself electrified, my spirits revive, my imagination warms, and my soul becomes susceptible of the softest and sublimest impressions. This

will

will not surprise you when I have only mentioned the objects which here present themselves to my view.

On the right is the hill of Posilipo, whose form is most agreeable; it is semi-circular, and adorned to the summit with trees and pleasure-houses; from its point, which loses itself in the sea, this mountain increases insensibly till it arrives behind the centre of Naples, and on its summit is seen a vast tower, which over-looks the city, and crowns the scene. On the left appears a chain of very high mountains which surround the other side of the gulph, and whose rugged boldness forms a most happy contrast with the elegant and cultivated beauties of Posilipo:—Shakspeare and Corneille would always have looked on

the

the side of Vesuvius; Racine and Pope on the side of Posilipo.

The Volcano is the most interesting of those mountains by its form which is a very beautiful cone, by its height, and above all by its vicinity to the city; it smokes incessantly, and seems always to threaten Naples with the fate of Sodom, to consume it with fire and brimstone. At its foot is Portici, and all along the coast are towns,* hanging from the mountains which form the portion of a circle of ninety miles.

The sea is under my window; and besides the ideas which it presents itself, as the most interesting object in nature next to the sun, by its grandeur, beauty, and the variety of

* Sorrento, one of those towns, is the country of Tasso.

its appearances, it here shews all the riches of commerce by large ships which are passing every moment. I often rise before day to enjoy the breath of the morning, and the superb description which the illustrious Rousseau gives of the rising of the sun. In no horizon does he appear with so much splendor, no where else does he so well deserve the epithet of *golden* *. He rises behind Vesuvius to illuminate the pleasant hill of Posilipo, and the bosom of the most beautiful gulph in the universe, smooth as a mirrour, and filled with vessels

---

* *Idcirco certis dimensum partibus orbem
Per duodena regit mundi Jol aureus astra.*

The golden sun, through twelve bright signs the year
Rules, and the earth in several climes divides.

all

all in motion. The object which terminates the perspective is the island of Capréa, famous for the retreat of Tiberius and the rocks of the Sirens: on viewing it, one remembers that near those rocks the prudent Ulyſſes ſtopped his ears; and that, not far from hence, the leſs wiſe Hannibal gave himſelf up to the pleaſures of harmony, and to the careſſes of the ſeducing Camilla.

LETTER XV.

Naples.

A FRENCHMAN is the moſt amiable of all men at home: why is he the leaſt liked in foreign countries? It is becauſe other nations are

are jealous of the superiority of the French, and because the French traveller behaves ill in the company of foreigners. Almost all the French who travel are young; they ridicule all customs but their own, and proclaim the vices and follies of a country in the midst of its assemblies. I was this evening at the *Academia de' Cavalieri,* where all the nobility of the country meet twice a week. Enters for the first time a young French marquis, whom I had known at Rome. Before he had been there two minutes he said to me, ' Did you ever see such ' animals? What a stupid look that ' man has! My God! how awkward ' that woman is! Did you ever see a ' head so horridly drest?' He said all this aloud; and even those who did

not

not underſtand him, ſaw by his manner that he deſpiſed them. The man who is going to execution will allow that he is a villain, that he deſerves the rack; but he will never allow that he deſerves contempt. The young Frenchman takes the ſureſt method that the wit of man can deviſe to make himſelf hated: this has always given me pain, becauſe I know that under this ſuperficial fault he conceals a thouſand good qualities; he is frivolous, light*, and ſelf-ſufficient, if you pleaſe; and that is the ſevereſt reproach his enemies can make him; but he is generous, he is frank, and he is always ready to draw his ſword

---

* Several French officers dining at Genoa with a nobleman of that city, one of them ſaid to him, "It is odd enough, Sir, that you are the "only ſtranger here."

in defence of his honour, of his miſtreſs, and of his friend. I ſhall be thought a Frenchman, and I am no Frenchman; I am an Engliſhman, and proud of being one; and at this moment I ſupport the character of my nation, and my own, by ſpeaking the language of truth and ſincerity, in repreſenting the French ſuch as I have found them.

In the arts, Italy is ſuperior to France and England: in the ſcience of war, the Germans have the advantage of the Engliſh and French; but, on the whole, theſe two nations are the firſt in Europe, and all other nations allow their ſuperiority. One circumſtance which pleaſed me in France, is, that the French always told me, that, next to their own, the

English nation was the moſt reſpectable: nothing but extravagant ſelf-love can oppoſe this deciſion: when the ſuffrages were collected at Athens, Ariſtides had the ſecond vote of all men; every one gave his firſt ſuffrage for himſelf. You, who are a rational being, ſet aſide your nation for a moment, and ſee how you would judge if the queſtion turned upon yourſelf: if a man ſhould ſay to you, ‘ I pre-‘ fer myſelf to you, but I prefer you ‘ to all other men;’ if you were not ſatisfied with this opinion, you would betray an immoderate ſelf-love, and a total ignorance of the human heart.

On my road hither, while the horſes were changing, I alighted to walk a few minutes: a Frenchman is not afraid of ſpeaking to his fellow crea-ture,

ture, and he soon finds a subject of conversation; an officer of dragoons of that nation, who was going to Rome, and was at the post-house, came up to me, ' You are an Englishman, Sir?' " At your service."—' Yours is a very ' respectable nation: I passed three ' years in England: you have depth ' and solidity; you are well bred, brave, ' magnificent'—" And the French, Sir?" —' They think too much to make ' themselves agreeable; they are too ' fond of levity, trifling, and amuse- ' ment: when a Frenchman travels, ' and loses his conceit and his foppish ' airs, and when an Englishman ac- ' quires a little softness and agreeable- ' ness in his behaviour, they become ' the first men in the world.'

I send

I send you what this gentleman said to me, because I think like him.

* * * *

P. S. The Abbé Galiani has the most wit of any man in Naples, and also the most learning; Duke Clement Filomarino is the poet who has the most talents and taste; his brother studies philosophy, and has a very improved mind; both of them are extremely amiable, and very well bred; their family seems to me the most respectable in the country. The Duke della Torre, their father, has the finest gallery of paintings here.

LETTER XVI.

NAPLES.

THE Neapolitans are really good people; but, in truth, they are very barbarous: they have adopted by inſtinct the principles of the citizen of Geneva, and they cultivate neither the arts nor ſciences, for fear of corrupting their morals. But if this nation is barbarous, do not think that it is harſh or ſevere, for, on the contrary, it is very good-natured, and deſirous of contributing to the pleaſure of foreigners: they are naturally good, but they are abſolutely in the ſtate in which nature produced them; and they perpetrate all crimes*, and

* I miſtake; a rape was never heard of at Naples.

are guilty of all forts of rudenefs, without thinking they have done ill. Having no education, they have no principle of any kind. A man of the firft quality will tread on your toes, and not make you the leaft apology: be acquainted with him the next day, he cannot do enough to oblige you; he will carry you to a concert, he will offer you his box at the theatre, he will do all he knows, but he knows little. It is the fame with the women; they have all an inclination to be amiable; it is a pity they don't know how.

'The race of Sirens * is not yet extinct here; there are many young women

---

* Thefe Sirens fometimes change into Harpies; but thefe metamorphofes feldom happen except in the magic land of the opera—

—*Virginci*

women who sing divinely: of Circes there are scarce any; but we see in the assemblies several of the companions of Ulysses. The easiness of the women and the *Scirocco* enervate the bodies of the men, and music enervates their souls, so as to render useless all the bounties which nature has lavished on this charming country. In no other place will be found more natural talents, or more circumstances favourable to the arts; but the causes above-mentioned, added to the indolence inspired by the climate, and the absolute want of Mæcenases,

― *Virginei vultus, fœdissima ventris
Proluvies, uncæque manus,*

With virgin faces, but with wombs obscene,
Foul paunches, and with ordure still unclean,
With claws for hands, and looks for ever lean.
Dryden.

cenafes, render Naples as favage as Ruffia; and a kind of proof of it is, that all the Ruffians who come hither are ftruck with the refemblance between the Neapolitans and their countrymen.

When a Neapolitan woman has no child, fhe is a very miferable being; for, having no refource in herfelf, fhe dies of *ennui:* when fhe has none, you may be fure it is not her fault, for the only idea which they have in their heads is that of love; and the only fubjects on which they can talk are their children, their nurfes, their lovers, or their hairdreffers. I have often regretted that thefe women have no knowledge, for whatever they know they tell with aftonifhing freedom and fimplicity. I was
fitting

sitting by one of them at their grand
assembly; I had seen her only once
before, but I had not spoken to her;
a *Soprano* had just finished an air,
and I said to the lady, 'That man
'has sung well.' "It is not a man,"
said she, "It is a *Musico*: he has sung
"very well, and he is the lover of
"that dutchess whom you see yon-
"der."—"Is it possible?"—"It is
"true; she has had a number of
"lovers, *Cavalieri, Cocchieri, Abbati**,
"at present she will have none but
"*Musici*." "Oh!" replied I, 'that is
'shameful!' "Yes," answered she,
"she is too inconstant;" *è troppo vola-
bile* was her phrase.

I asked another, whom I had known
some time, how many lovers she had,

* Gentlemen, Coachmen, Abbés.

four

four or five? She assured me, with a most serious air, that she had not had one for three weeks. Do not be surprised at my question to this lady, it was in order to make my court to her: A Neapolitan lady is vain of the number of her adorers; and I have seen some come into company with a train of five. In general, there are not more than two of them that are the well-beloved; the others are only kept as slaves for parade.

P. S. I think, that when I marry, I shall chuse an ugly wife, that, if I should lose her, I may be sure to recover her. My dog has been sent me: what rejoicings on both sides!

O qui complexus, O gaudia quanta fuere!

LETTER

LETTER XVII.

NAPLES.

THE king of Spain said that " every prince of the house of 'Bourbon must be passionately fond 'of women or of hunting:' his Sicilian majesty is very fond of hunting;' he scarce passes a day in the midst of summer, or in the sharpest colds of winter, without partaking of it. During my residence at Naples, he retired for two months to Caserta, on purpose to hunt, which gave concern to all the English, as that deprived us of the society and house of Sir William Hamilton, who went also to Caserta, for the king never goes a hunting without him; and he is so

fond

fond of the company of that minifter, that it was with difficulty he obtained leave from his majefty to come for one day only to Naples to give a dinner to his countrymen: I dined there the forty-fixth Englifhman.

If I fay nothing to you concerning Vefuvius, it is becaufe Sir William Hamilton has left nothing to be defired on that fubject. His letters, more fatisfactory than thofe of Pliny, will inftruct you in a fhort time, and with pleafure: they are written with clearnefs and precifion, and with that noble fimplicity which diftinguifhes their author in all the fituations of life.

During the ftay at Caferta, the queen loft her eldeft fon; he was a prince of five years of age, a charming boy.

boy. Her majesty was in the eighth month of her pregnancy; twenty-four hours before his death, she had been assured that he was out of danger; you may judge how severe a stroke this must be to a tender mother; and she was very near sinking under it. These circumstances alone were sufficiently trying; but there was one dreadful moment which all but killed her. The young prince had seemed better for a day, but all on a sudden he was seized with a convulsion fit: one of his women, a German, as she was running to call assistance, hit her head against a door half open, gave herself a large wound in her forehead, and fell backward in a swoon: the convulsions increased, and a second woman, a German also, ran to hasten the

the physician; on her way she found
the first woman in a swoon and covered
with blood; she thought her dead,
and the fright made her also fall into
a swoon: the wind was very high,
and, by what accident is not known,
the roof of the prince's house took
fire; the queen arrived at that instant, found these two women in this
situation, her son in agonies, and the
palace in flames. Half an hour after
the prince died *.

LET-

* Every step of my travels has given me fresh occasion to admire the truth with which Shakspeare has painted all the objects in nature, and all the situations of human life. The queen afflicted herself for several days; and a lady of the court told me that she often exclaimed, "Ah! "if my son had not been pretty, my loss would "have been less severe; but it was the most "charming child!" These are almost word for word the same expressions which Shakspeare has made a queen in *King John* utter in the same situation:

" Con-

LETTER XVIII.

Rome.

THERE is not a river in Europe less beautiful than the Tiber, nor a character in history more dreadful than that of Augustus. There is however no river whose sight is more interesting; and few names inspire more admiration than that of this emperor. For this let both of them

---

" *Constance.* Had he been ugly,
Lame, foolish, crooked, swart, prodigious,
Patch'd with foul moles, and eye-offending marks,
I would not care, I then would be content:
But since the birth of Cain, the first male-child,
To him that did but yesterday suspire,
There was not such a *gracious creature* born."
And a little after,
  " Therefore never, never
Must I behold my *pretty* Arthur more.'

thank Horace and Virgil; it is owing to the choice of their language, and to the harmony of their verſes, that the Tiber is not ſeen with difguſt, and that the name of Auguſtus does not infpire us with horror and ſadneſs. How ſenſible has the Great Frederick been of this truth! and with how much addreſs has he attached thoſe French and Italian writers who will be read with the greateſt pleaſure as long as theſe two languages exiſt! In a thouſand years the cries of widows, and the complaints of orphans, will be no longer heard; all the horrors which his wars have occaſioned will be forgotten; and nothing will remain of him but the rapid and irreſiſtible conqueror, the juſt and beneficent king, the patron of learning and arts, the great poet, the profound philosopher, the able politician, and the amiable companion, who was the delight of the choicest society of his age.

The king of Prussia has never thought but of futurity, and he has insured the admiration of posterity by his poetry, by his prose, and by his actions. But how has he taken care to fortify his triple immortality by the graces of a Voltaire, and the elegance of an Algarotti! You may see by what he makes Glory say to a sage who had gained her temple, that this divinity has always been the sole object of his worship:

La Déesse, approuvant l'effort de son courage,
Lui dit, " Soyez heureux, jouïssez du partage
" De ces esprits actifs, auteurs, rois, et guerriers;
" Le repos est permis, mais c'est sous des lauriers."

The goddess, with his courage pleas'd,
" Be happy," cried, " the lot enjoy
" Of those brave spirits, authors, warriors,
    kings;
" Repose you may, but in a laurel shade."

His ode on glory shews both the fire of his imagination, and the ruling passion of his soul;

Take the first lines;

Un Dieu s'empare de mon ame,
  Je sens un céleste ardeur;
O Gloire! ta divine flamme
  M' embrase jusq'au fond de la cœur.

A Deity my soul invades,
  A warmth divine I feel;
O Glory! thy celestial flame
  My heart's recesses burns.

And the last stanza;

O Gloire! à qui je sacrifie
  Mes plaisirs et mes passions,
O Gloire! en qui je me confie,
  Daigne éclairer mes actions:

Tu peux, malgré la mort cruelle,
Sauver une foible etincelle
 De l'esprit qui réside en moi.
Que ta main m'ouvre la barriere;
Et prêt à courir ta carriere,
 Je veux vivre et mourir pour toi.

Glory! to whom I sacrifice
 My pleasures and my passions too,
Glory! in whom I trust, O deign
 To set my deeds in perfect day:
Thou of the spirit, that resides
Within this clay, one feeble spark,
 In spite of cruel death, canst save.
O let thy hand the gate unbar,
And, ready thy career to run,
 I'll live and die for thee.

LETTER XIX.

ROME.

AT Rome, as well as in all the other countries that I have seen, the French houses are the most agreeable.

able. The Cardinal de Bernis has a large affembly once a week, and he gives a dinner every day. The Bailiff de la Brillanne, ambaffador from Malta, alfo frequently gives dinners; he is very affable, and has an excellent cook. His brother had fent him a fervice of china, which was made on purpofe for him, with his arms; an Englifh frigate took the French fhip in which was the china, and the lofs was the more grievous as he was the ambaffador of a neutral power. Three days after his receiving this news, I had the honour to dine with him, and he loaded me with civilities: I mention this as a ftroke that characterifes his nation.

Of all the great affemblies here, that of Monfeigneur de Bayanne, auditor

ditor of the rota of France, has the moſt amuſements; a table of *Bocetti* in one room; in another literature, politics, news, are the ſubjects of diſcourſe; and in a third, you will find one of the beſt concerts in Italy, a ſuperb orcheſtra, and the firſt ſingers of both ſexes in Rome. You will find at his dinners French fare, French gaiety, French politeneſs. The maſter of the houſe is truly amiable; I only find one fault in him, and that is not generally the fault of a Frenchman; he is more fond of hearing than of talking. One ſees that this is owing to his extreme politeneſs, but one don't ſuffer the leſs, as he never opens his mouth but to ſay ſomething agreeable or profound. A Frenchman talks better than other men;

men; I have not known one of his countrymen exprefs themfelves with more purity, more clearnefs, or more elegance: his tafte in letters is fure: I have feen few perfons in my travels fo interefting as he is.

Colonel de Bayanne, his brother, is polite, agreeable, good-natured: he loves the arts, and amufes himfelf with painting very pretty pictures.

Does it appear to you to be of little importance that I point out to you what is moft interefting in a country, and that I fave you the trouble and the time of difcovering it yourfelf? Be fure then not to leave Rome without being introduced to the Marchionefs de Bocca-Paduli: her affembly is the moft agreeable and the beft chofen in Rome: among

other

other persons of merit you will there meet the Count de Verri, a Milanese* gentleman, who is full of politeness, taste, and talents: The lady of the house will please you extremely, for she is witty, well-made, and amiable as a Frenchwoman.

I have pleasure in speaking of persons whom I can praise with truth: Here then follows an English lady, who has done great execution here and at Naples: she has vivacity and uncommon judgment; has read much, and assumes nothing: I have scarce seen a young lady so well educated, or so desirous of instruction. She speaks Italian well, French perfectly; she is passionately fond of paintings

* I must tell you here, in regard to the Milanese, that the Lombard heart is proverbially good in Italy.

and

and antiquities, and she draws very prettily; but her most diftinguished accomplishment is mufic: Millico, who has the moft tafte of any finger in Italy, has been her mafter; and she has profited by his inftructions fo much, that I have feen her feveral times enchant the moft critical judges of Rome and Naples.

I met a young Frenchman at Turin, who had heard her fing at Rome, and who was a paffionate admirer of the Italian mufic; I afked him how he liked her? This was his anfwer:

J'entends encore fa voix, ce langage enchanteur,
Et ces fons fouverains de l'oreille et du cœur.

Her voice, th' enchanting language, ftill I hear,
Thofe fovereign accents of the heart and ear.

* It is certain that the Italian is a divine language for poetry and mufic; it is better to fing than to fpeak: the French language is much more rapid and precife.

Add

Add to these talents, a charming shape; a most elegant and graceful manner, a complexion of a dazzling white, animated by the most beautiful carnation in the world, two eyes full of softness and spirit, and seventeen years of age, and you have the portrait of Lady Louisa Nugent.

Perhaps you may be tempted to suspect that this is a fancy-piece rather than a copy from nature. I assure you it is as true a portrait as ever was painted by Titian or Vandyck; and the proof of it is that this young lady captivated three nations; the Italians were enchanted with her, '*aveva tanto briö, et tante buone maniere**;' the French, '*elle*

---

* ' She had so much vivacity and politeness.'

'*étoit*

'*étoit si jolie et si aimable*†;' and the English, '*she was so modest and so sensible.*'

LETTER XX.

ROME.

I Frequented the men of letters here, as I do every where, particularly the poets. It is incredible, that with such parts as the Italians have, they should be so much behind other nations in their poetical knowledge: they have an obstinate blindness in favour of their poets, of which I do not think they will ever be cured. The *Bolge* of Dante, and the extravagances of Ariosto, are the objects of

* 'She was so pretty and so amiable.'

their

their idolatry; and, in spite of reason and common sense, they prefer those absurdities to the finest productions of all other nations. Dante, according to them, is the first of all men; and Ariosto, whom they own to be inferior to Dante, is infinitely above Homer. After having read the *Divina Comedia*, and the *Orlando Furioso*, I began to give my opinion of them according to the ideas established in my country *, in France, and in all

places

[* It is by no means so decided a point as this author ventures to assert, that Dante and Ariosto are not ranked among the first of poets even 'in 'this country;' and if in some well-known passages the former has equalled any poet of any age, his abilities must be allowed equal to his best lines. Ariosto, however, adopts a different plan; ridicule, satire, wit, and humour, with every romantic extravagance of an unconfined genius, an imagination without controul, and almost without equal, spread such a variety over his work,

that

places where there are men of taste. I spoke the language of reason, the
Italian

that no reader can be weary through the lecture of XLVI Cantos, and while romance and whim declare the poem often comic rather than heroic, there are parts which no human power has ever yet excelled, as muſt be acknowledged by the impartial judge, who will, in ſpite of modern fine-drawn criticiſm, avow his real feelings through the riſe and progreſs of Orlando's madneſs, for which the whole ſeems to have been written; the reader is led on with the enamoured hero, by degrees feels all his weight of woes, and ſcarcely wonders at any extravagance they produce. No poet has more naturally, more pathetically, painted every ſtage and every effect of that incomprehenſible diſtemper ravaging a ſtrong mind in a moſt athletic body. In other parts every other paſſion may be found as well diſplayed; and in the character of Bradamante, in particular, every virtue, every charm, that can captivate a reader, for womanhood, in her moſt amiable appearance, is, with every refinement of ſentiment, preſerved through the whole character; and each character ſtands in the work as preciſely diſtinguiſhed from all others as even thoſe of Homer. The faults which none dare juſtify, and none can deſire to excuſe, are where indecent and groſs ideas are let looſe on the

reader,

Italian poets were not used to it; they declared war against me: I quitted their

reader, but with so much wit, humour, and vivacity, that no one, it is supposed, ever could stop and pass over his exceptionable cantos, though the whimsical author warns his reader, and particularly announces to the fair, that they should not and need not read such passages. And, after all, it has been suggested, particularly by the late ingenious Mr. Hawkins Browne, with great appearance of probability, that the whole design of the author was to ridicule romances, and that he is in heroic poetry what Cervantes is in prose; and that even the Italians, who almost idolise their Furioso, saw not that admirable design throughout the whole performance, which alone can excuse the extravagant flights and comic absurdities every where interspersed, while the genius that gives these proofs of a most powerful imagination, proves likewise that he had power to have elevated his poem to any height he had chosen. Mr. Browne, who was an excellent judge, because he was superior to all little prejudices and minute criticisms, held Ariosto in the highest estimation, and ranked him with the first of Italian poets. For wherever the pathetic, the animated, the terrible, the descriptive, or the plaintive, give opportunities for the Muse to expatiate, her powers are unquestionable.

their society; and I thought I should do service to poetry, by publishing a book in Italian *, in which I endeavoured to shew young poets the principles on which they ought to compose: I told them that nature and truth were the only basis of poetry; that the Greek authors were the best models on which a young poet could form himself; that France also had some excellent authors; that Racine was as good a model as Sophocles;

nable. And no less warm was this candid judge in his encomiums on Metastasio, of whose extensive genius, and chastity of style and sentiment, he had the highest opinion; and for the fertility of his imagination, and the pointed strength of his sentiments, Mr. Browne styled him the Shakspeare of Italy! It is also observable, that his language is clearer to a foreigner, and easier to be understood by a learner of Italian, than any other poet of that country, which is an undoubted proof of the purity and perfection of his poetry.]

* *Consiglio ad un giovane Poeta.*

that

that Greece had not a fabulist equal to La Fontaine, nor a comic poet so perfect as Moliere; that Horace, Longinus, and Boileau, were the best critics that ever existed, and that nothing which was not conformable to their principles was good. I sought only the progress of the art among men who are full of genius, and who have a divine poetical language, but who know not what to do either with the one or the other. I allowed that these three critics would have been charmed with the beauties of Dante and Ariosto, taken from nature, and founded on truth; but that they would have condemned the whole of those two poems, as being contrary to reason, good sense, and consequently to good taste, and, as models,

models, dangerous to an extreme for young poets.

My book procured me some votes and many reproaches; the poets took the alarm; they cried that the true taste of the Italian poetry would perish, if attention were given to an *Ultramontain* (a term synonymous with them to that of barbarian).

There were so many persons who exclaimed, and they exclaimed so loudly, that I myself was beginning almost to believe that my book was good for nothing; when one morning I found an extract of it in the *Efféméridi Letterarie* of Rome, with some remarks which did it justice; this gave me the more pleasure, as I was an utter stranger to it till that moment, and as the article was there inserted

K by

by the Count de Bianconi, minister from the court of Dresden, well known for his taste and talents: with this suffrage, I had ten or twelve more; that was a great deal, if you consider that at Naples I had only four: at Rome there are 200,000 inhabitants; at Naples 400,000: in those two cities I found about sixteen persons who admitted nature and truth to be the foundation of poetry, and who acknowledged Horace, Longinus, and Boileau, to be judges: of this small number, the Abbé Scarpelli, whom you have heard mentioned as one of the best poets of the Arcadia, was one: this is a sonnet which he sent me, and which I insert here, lest you should not have seen it at the end of the third edition of my book, where it is placed.

ALL'

ALL' ERUDITISSIMO *Signor* SHERLOCK.

SONETTO.

Chi pon silenzio in Pindo al turbin roco
   Di vuoti di ragion carmi sonanti?
Chi sull' are del gusto avviva il foco
   Dal cener freddo che premealo innanti?

Sei tu, saggio SHERLOCK, che prese a gioco
   Le magic' opre e i favolosi incanti,
Fai che a NATURA e a VERITA dian loco
   L'alte follie de' Paladini erranti:

Tu dissipi i Danteschi orror segreti,
   Che in Ausonia finor culto divino
Ebber dai troppo creduli Poeti;

Onde il guardo volgendo al suol Latino
   Flacco e Boileau, fatti per te più lieti;
Ecco, gridano, Italia, il tuo Longino.

     Dell' Abbate Antonio Scarpelli,
        Sotto-Custode d'Arcadia in Roma.

Imité

Imité librement.

Qui fait taire ces sons qu'un vain delire enfante?
Qui rallume du gout le flambeau pâliffant?
C'eft toi, SHERLOCK; par toi la raifon triomphante
Voit deja parmi nous fon culte renaiffant.

Epris du Ferrarois, fon exemple infidele,
Egaroit notre efprit fur fa trace emporté;
Ton ouvrage à nos yeux offre un autre modele
Celui de la NATURE et de la VERITE'.

Horace en tes écrits reconnoit fon génie,
Defpréaux applaudit à ton goût fûr et fin;
Tous deux ont dit, "O bords de l'antique Aufonie,
Bords heureux, vous auffi, vous avez un Longin."

To the moft learned Signor SHÉRLOCK.

SONNET.

On Pindus' fummit who allays the ftorms,
    The empty reafoning, of melodious bards?
Who on the rock of tafte thus nobly warms
    The frozen afhes, wont to claim rewards?

'Tis

'Tis thou, sage SHERLOCK, who hast taught our
   youth
Of magic and romance to spurn the flights,
Triumphant long o'er NATURE and o'er TRUTH
   In the mad follies of advent'rous knights:
Thou Dante's secret horrors canst disperse,
Crown'd in Ausonia by the sons of verse,
   Too weak and credulous, with wreaths divine:
Whence turning to the Latian shore, we see
Horace, Boileau, made more renown'd by thee;
   A new Longinus, Italy, is thine.

   The Abbé Antonio Scarpelli,
      Under-keeper of the Arcadia in Rome.

You have here a great deal of me and my book: but allowance must be made for the vanity of an author: I always had self-love enough, and since I am printed, I perceive I have much more.

LETTER XXI.

ROME.

Je ne vous paffe rien fi vous n'êtes Grand Homme;
Unlefs you're great, I will forgive you nothing;

THAT is well faid, and it is a great man who fays it: But if you are a great man—one ought to blufh at being able to difcover an expletive in Corneille, or a pun in Shakfpeare, when both are furrounded by a crowd of beauties: this is one of the fubjects on which I have had occafion to be diffatisfied with the French; they were always calumniating Shakfpeare, and I fhould have fuffered much lefs if they had attacked myfelf. Nature never produced a poet equal to him; Homer approaches the neareft to him, but at a great * diftance: you fmile; but a moment ago, fay you, I condemned the Italians for the extravagance of their prejudices in favour of Dante; and now I am guilty of the fame crime, and from the fame caufe, an excefs of national felf-love. I did not prefume to condemn Dante on my own ideas: much lefs do I prefume to exalt Shakfpeare on my own judgement: I would not admit the Italians as judges of Dante, nor the Englifh as judges of Shakfpeare; I fummon them both to the tribunal of Longinus, Horace, and Boileau; and I would have each of them hold the rank which fhall be granted him by the united decifion of thofe critics.

* *Proximus . . . fed longo proximus intervallo.*

It would be wronging me to think that I would exclude a nation from judging of its own poets. When men have their taste formed on sure principles, those of the same country are unquestionably the best judges of their authors; but a Russian, well acquainted with the poets and critics of Greece, Rome, and France, would judge with more certainty of the merit of Racine, than a Parisian, born with equal talents, but who had not cultivated them.

Thus it was that I reasoned with the French in favour of Shakspeare: an English youth goes to school at eight years of age; he stays there till sixteen; he then passes five years at the university: during that time he only studies the Greek, Latin, and French

French authors, and the sciences; for an Englishman does not make a study of his own language, the only essential defect in his education. At the age then of one-and-twenty, deeply read in the ancient authors, and with his taste formed on the principles of Horace, Longinus, and Boileau; he begins to read Shakspeare; the English nation is reckoned to have judgment, and this is their education; in two hundred years, there has not been a single voice in this country against this poet: I then quoted to them this passage of Longinus, in the words of Boileau: " When in a great number
" of persons of different professions
" and ages every one has been affected
" in the same manner, this uniform
" opinion and approbation of so many
" minds,

"minds, in other respects so discordant, is a certain and undoubted proof that there is there something of the marvellous and the great."

All this did not convince them; a Frenchman does not like reasoning; he has always answered me by a *bon mot*.

The enlightened Italians will own, allowing all the merit of Dante, that his poem is the worst that there is in any language: when we think of the age in which he lived, the poet must be deemed a prodigy; when we read his poem at present, it must be considered as a mass of various kinds of knowledge gothickly heaped together, without order and without design. Take away from the *Divine Comedy* five or six beautiful passages, and

and four or five hundred fine verſes, what remains is only a tiſſue of barbariſms, abſurdities, and horrors.

And had not Shakſpeare faults? He had many and great ones: he wrote ten volumes of plays, he wrote for the ſtage, and he was obliged to flatter the taſte of his age, which was bad.—Therefore the merit of Shakſpeare and that of Dante are equal; they both had ſublime beauties and great faults:—There is only this difference, that the grand paſſages of the Italian poet are reducible to the narration of Count Ugolino, the hiſtory of Franceſca di Rimini, the deſcription of the arſenal of Venice, and two or three more; and that the grand paſſages of Shakſpeare are innumerable; that in Dante we ſhall find,

find, in three pages, four beautiful lines; and that in Shakſpeare we ſhall find, in four pages, ſix lines that are not beautiful.

This poet gained by his talents the patronage of ſovereigns, and the friendſhip of nobles; he was celebrated with emulation by all the poets his contemporaries and his ſucceſſors; an inconteſtable proof that a genius ſo rare was even ſuperior to envy.

The beſt pieces of Shakſpeare have faults; but each of his good ones ſeems to me to reſemble the church of St. Peter: this temple, the moſt wonderful in the world, has a thouſand faults, a thouſand bad things in ſculpture, painting, &c. &c. but I pity the man who thinks of looking for

for them: when a fault presents itself, let him advance a step farther, sublime beauty expects him.

These ideas struck me this morning while I was walking in this church: I went thither with a Pole, a Frenchman, and an Englishman: the Englishman looked for beauties; the Frenchman for faults; the Pole looked for nothing. When we were at the end of the church, 'Behold,' says the Frenchman, ' that *Charity* ' of Bernini, how wretched it is! the ' air of her head is affected, her flesh ' is without bone, and she makes ' frightful faces.' " These remarks " appear to me just enough," replies the Englishman, " but, look on the " other side of the altar, you will " see one of the finest pieces of mo-
" dern

"dern sculpture, the *Justice* of Guglielmo della Porta." 'You are in the right,' says the Frenchman (without looking at it), 'but that child at the foot of the *Charity* disgusts me more than its mother.' While the Englishman continued to praise the *Justice*, and the Frenchman to criticise the *Charity*, the Pole looked at the door by which we entered, and said to me, that 'the church was much longer than he imagined.'

In passing under the dome, the boldness of Michael Angelo reminded me of the imagination of Shakspeare; and the successive impressions made on me by the Justice, the Charity, the St. Michael of Guido, the St. Jerom of Dominichino, and the Transfiguration

figuration of Raphael, were similar to those which I have often felt in reading Othello, &c. The Frenchman's delicacy often degenerates into squeamishness; he is too easily offended; and he suffers more pain from one fault than he enjoys pleasure from ten beauties. I am the friend of reason and exactness as much as Boileau was; but I can pardon some faults which are compensated by numerous and sublime beauties:

Je ne vous passe rien si vous n'êtes Grand Homme,

is the language of the King of Prussia; it is also that of Longinus; and, lest you should have forgotten the passage, take it as follows:

"It is almost impossible for a middling genius to commit faults; for as

" as he ventures nothing, and never
" rises, he remains in safety; instead
" of which, the great man, of him-
" self, and by his own greatness,
" slips and is in danger.——Though I
" have remarked many faults in
" Homer, and in all the most cele-
" brated authors, and though I am
" perhaps the man in the world
" whom they please the least, I reckon
" that these are faults which they
" did not regard, and negligences
" which escaped them, because their
" genius, which only studied the
" great, could not dwell on little
" matters. In a word, I maintain
" that the sublime, though it does
" not support itself equally through-
" out, prevails over all the rest. In
" Theocritus, there is nothing but
" what

"what is happily imagined; but will you therefore fay that Theocritus is a greater poet than Homer, who wants order and contrivance in feveral paffages of his writings; but who commits this fault only on account of that divine fpirit which hurries him away, and which he cannot regulate as he would." Ah! if Longinus had read Shakfpeare!

This principle is in like manner fupported by Horace;

—*Ubi plura nitent in carmine*—

As in Shakfpeare,

Non ego paucis offendar maculis;

In a work where many beauties fhine,
I will not cavil at a few miftakes:

And by the bye,

Ubi pauca nitent in carmine,

as in Dante, I will not suffer myself to be dazzled by some shreds of purple *.

We should have little enjoyment in the contemplation of the arts, or of nature, if we always looked for an exemption from faults. I do not ask any indulgence for Carlo Maratti; but woe to the man who cannot pardon a defect of contour in Rubens or Corregio!

LETTER XXII.

FROM THE MIDDLE OF THE ALPS.

I passed these mountains with a young Frenchman, who was passionately fond of the Italian music: when we arrived at our inn, we went to take a walk

* *Purpureus pannus.*

a walk on the side of a small lake, surrounded by a delightful wood: '*Parbleu*,' said he, ' Nature is very ' ridiculous here.'—" Ha!" replied I, " this is something new: I have often " heard of the caprices of nature, but " you are the first who have found " her ridiculous."—' Listen!' said he; (the wood resounded with the song of nightingales, and the lake was full of frogs that were croaking) ' have ' you ever heard such a concert?'— " Yes, I have heard some Frenchmen " and Italian women sing together." He took the joke in good part, and we laughed at the ridiculousness of nature, and of the opera-singers at Paris.

From the date of this letter you expect, no doubt, something sublime on the Alps, on Hannibal, or Livy: Not a word; it is another volume of my letters, which I am going to announce to you, on the northern parts of Italy, which are much more cultivated in every respect than those of the south, on the other German courts, &c. &c. But lest I should not fulfil this threat, let me tell you at present, that of all the princes whom I have seen, he that pleases me the most is Prince * Ernest of Mecklenburgh-Strelitz; and that Venice seems to me the Athens of Italy. You have a fine opportunity of determining this last idea in *the Tribune* at Florence, by comparing the Venus of Titian with that of Medicis; examine them both with attention, and you will

[* Third brother to the Queen of England.]

allow

allow that no impartial perſon can prefer the work of the Grecian artiſt to that of the Venetian *. If you wiſh to have other proofs, I cite the general turn of mind and manners of the inhabitants; and I add to the name of Titian thoſe of Palladio, Maffei, and Algarotti.

As to Prince Erneſt, I think him every thing that can be deſired in a prince; and if you would have a proof of that, go to Zell.

[* But, it may be aſked, how can a ſtatue be well compared with a picture, eſpecially of a maſter whoſe drawing is generally thought defective, and whoſe chief excellence is his colouring? and beſides, the Venus of Titian, I apprehend, is cumbent.]

LETTER XXIII.

FERNEY, *April* 26, 1776*.

THE Marquis d'Argens, of Angoulême, gave me a letter to M. de Voltaire, with whom he is intimately acquainted. Every one recommended by M. d'Argens is sure to be well received at Ferney: M. de Voltaire treated me with great civility; my first visit lasted two hours, and he invited me to dinner the next day. Each day, when I left him, I went to an inn, where I wrote down the most remarkable things that he had said to me; here they are.

* The reader sees the reason why I have not placed my letters in chronological order; and if he does not see it, it is no matter.

He met me in the hall; his nephew, M. d'Hornois, counfellor in the parliament of Paris, held him by the arm; he faid to me, with a very weak voice, " You fee a very old " man, who makes a great effort to " have the honour of feeing you; " will you take a walk in my gar- " den? It will pleafe you, for it is " in the Englifh tafte; it was I who " introduced that tafte into France, " and it is become univerfal; but the " French parody your gardens, they " put thirty acres in three."

From his gardens you fee the Alps, the Lake, the city of Geneva, and its environs, which are very pleafant. He faid, " *It is a beautiful profpect:*" he pronounced thefe words tolerably well.

S. How

S. How long is it since you were in England?

V. Fifty years at least.

His Nephew. It was at the time when you printed the first edition of your Henriade.

We then talked of literature; and from that moment he forgot his age and infirmities, and spoke with the warmth of a man of thirty. He said some shocking things against Moses and against Shakspeare.

V. Shakspeare is detestably translated by M. de la Place. He has substituted de la Place to Shakspeare. I have translated the three first acts of Julius Cæsar with exactness: a translator should lose his own genius, and assume that of his author. If the author be a buffoon, the translator should

should be so too: Shakspeare always had a buffoon; it was the taste of the age, which he took from the Spaniards: the Spaniards had always a buffoon; sometimes it was a god, sometimes a devil; sometimes he prayed, at other times he fought.

We talked of Spain.

V. It is a country of which we know no more than of the most savage parts of Africa, and it is not worth the trouble of being known. If a man would travel there, he must carry his bed, &c. When he comes into a town, he must go into one street to buy a bottle of wine, a piece of a mule in another, he finds a table in a third, and he sups. A French nobleman was passing through Pampeluna: he sent out for a spit; there was

was only one in the town, and that was borrowed for a wedding.

His Nephew. That is a village which M. de Voltaire has built!

V. Yes; we are free here; cut off a little corner, and we are out of France. I asked some privileges for my children here, and the king has granted me all that I asked, and has declared the country of Gex free from all the taxes of the farmers-general; so that salt, which formerly sold for ten sols a pound, now sells for four. I have nothing more to ask—except to live.

We went into the library.

V. There are several of your countrymen (he had Shakspeare, Milton, Congreve, Rochester, Shaftesbury, Bolingbroke, Robertson, Hume, &c.) Robertson

Robertson is your Livy; his Charles V. is written with truth. Hume wrote his history to be applauded, Rapin to instruct; and both obtained their ends.

S. You knew lord Chesterfield?

V. Yes, I knew him; he had a great deal of wit.

S. You know lord Hervey*?

V. I have the honour to correspond with him.

S. He has talents.

V. As much wit as Lord Chesterfield, and more solidity.

S. Lord Bolingbroke and you agreed that we have not one good tragedy.

V. True; Cato is incomparably well written: Addison had much taste, but the abyss between taste and genius is immense. Shakspeare had an amazing

* Now Earl of Bristol.

genius,

genius, but no taſte; he has ſpoiled the taſte of the nation; he has been their taſte for two hundred years; and what is the taſte of a nation for two hundred years, will be ſo for two thouſand: this taſte becomes a religion; and there is in your country a great many fanatics in regard to Shakſpeare.

S. Were you perſonally acquainted with Lord Bolingbroke?

V. Yes; his face was impoſing, and ſo was his voice; in his works there are many leaves, and little fruit; diſtorted expreſſions, and periods intolerably long.

" There," ſaid he, " you ſee the " Alcoran, which is well read at leaſt:" it was marked throughout with bits of paper: " there are *Hiſtoric Doubts* " by Horace Walpole" (which had alſo
ſeveral

several marks) "here is the portrait
"of Richard III *; you see, he was a
"handsome youth."

S. You have built a church?

V. True; and it is the only one in
the universe in honour of God †; you
have churches built to St. Paul, to
St Genevieve, but not one to God.

This is what he said to me the
first day. You did not expect any
connection in this dialogue, because I
only put down the most striking things
that he said. I have perhaps mangled
some of his phrases; but, as well as
I can recollect, I have given his own
words.

* In the frontispiece, [drawn by Vertue and
engraved by Grignion. Mr. Walpole purchased
this drawing at Vertue's sale. Whence it was
taken is not known, probably from some painted
window.]

† The inscription was, *Deo erexit Voltaire.*

LETTER XXIV.

FERNEY.

THE next day, as we sat down to dinner, he said, "We are here *for liberty and property* *. This gentleman † is a Jesuit, he wears his hat: I am a poor invalid, I wear my night-cap."

I do not immediately recollect why he quoted these verses:

> Here lies the mutton-eating king,
>   Whose promise none relies on,
> Who never said a foolish thing,
>   Nor ever did a wise one ‡.

---

* In English.
† Father Adam.
[‡ Lord Rochester on King Charles II.]

But, speaking of Racine, he quoted these two;

The weighty bullion of one sterling line,
Drawn to French wire would through whole
    pages shine *.

S. The English prefer Corneille to Racine.

V. That is because the English are not sufficiently acquainted with the French tongue to feel the beauties of Racine's style, or the harmony of his versification: Corneille ought to please them more, because he is more striking; but Racine pleases the French, because he has more softness and tenderness.

S. How did you find the English fare †?   *V.* Very

[* Lord Roscommon's Essay on Translated Verse. English Poets, vol. X. p. 215.]
[† In the original it is, " Comment avez vous " trouvé la *chere* Angloise" [the English *cheer*].
                                    Voltaire

V. Very frefh and very white.

It fhould be remembered, that when he made this pun upon women, he was in his eighty-third year.

S. Their language?

V. Energic, precife, and barbarous; they are the only nation that pronounces their A, E.

He related an anecdote of Swift: " Lady Carteret, wife of the Lord " Lieutenant of Ireland in Swift's " time, faid to him, The air of this " country is good." Swift fell down on his knees, ' For God's fake, madam, ' don't fay fo in England; they will ' certainly tax it.'

He afterwards faid, that.." though " he could not perfectly pronounce

Voltaire jocularly anfwers as if it were '*chair*, ' flefh.' The tranflator has endeavoured to retain the pun.]

" Englifh,

" English, his ear was sensible of the
" harmony of their language and of
" their versification; that Pope and
" Dryden had the most harmony in
" poetry, Addison in prose."

V. How have you found the French?

S. Amiable and witty: I only find one fault with them; they imitate the English too much.

V. How! do you think us worthy to be originals ourselves?

S. Yes, Sir.

V. So do I too; but it is of your government that we are jealous.

S. I have found the French more free than I expected.

V. Yes, as to walking, or eating whatever he pleases, or lolling in his elbow-chair, a Frenchman is free enough; but as to taxes—Ah! Sir, you are happy, you may do any thing; we are born in flavery, and we die in flavery; we cannot even die as we will, we muſt have a prieſt.

Speaking of our government, he ſaid, " the Engliſh ſell themſelves, " which is a proof that they are " worth ſomething: we French do " not ſell ourſelves; probably becauſe " we are worth nothing."

S. What is your opinion of the Eloïſe?

V. It will not be read twenty years hence.

S. Mademoiſelle de l'Enclos has written good letters.

V. She never wrote one; they were by the wretched Crebillon.

" The Italians," he ſaid, " were a " nation of brokers; that Italy was
" an

" an old wardrobe, in which there
" were many old cloaths of exquisite
" taste. We are still," said he, " to
" know whether the subjects of the
" Pope or of the Grand Turk are the
" most abject."

He talked of England and of Shakspeare; and explained to Madam Denis
part of a scene in Henry V, where the
King makes love to Queen Catherine
in bad French, and of another in
which that Queen takes a lesson in
English from her waiting-woman, and
where there are several very gross
double-entendres, particularly on the
word '*foot*;' and then addressing himself to me, " But see," said he, " what
" it is to be an author; he will do any
" thing to get money."

V. When I see an Englishman sub-
tle

tle and fond of law-suits, I say, 'There is a Norman, who came in with William the Conqueror!' When I see a man good-natured and polite, 'that is one who came with the Plan-tagenets;' a brutal character, 'that is a Dane;' for your nation, as well as your language, is a medley of many others.

After dinner, passing through a little parlour, where there was a head of Locke, another of the Countess of Coventry, and several more, he took me by the arm, and stopped me —" Do you know this bust*; it is "the greatest genius that ever ex-"isted: if all the geniuses of the "universe were assembled, he should "lead the band."

* It was the bust of Newton.

It

It was of Newton, and of his own works, that he always spoke with the greatest warmth.

LETTER XXV.

IF you have not time to read a short detail of trifling circumstances relating to Voltaire, pass this letter.

His house is convenient, and well furnished; among other pictures is the portrait of the Empress of Russia, and that of the King of Prussia, which was sent him by that monarch, as was also his own bust in Berlin porcelain, with the inscription IMMORTALIS.

His arms are on his door, and on all his plates, which are of silver: at the desert, the spoons, forks, and blades

blades of the knives, were of filver gilt: there were two courfes, and five fervants, three of whom were in livery: no ftrange fervant is allowed to enter.

He fpends his time in reading, writing, playing at chefs with Father Adam, and in looking at the workmen building in his village.

The foul of this extraordinary man has been the theatre of every ambition: he wifhed to be a univerfal writer; he wifhed to be rich; he wifhed to be noble; and he has fucceeded in all.

His laft ambition was to found a town; and if we examine, we fhall find that all his ideas tended to this point. After the difgrace of M. de Choifeul, when the French miniftry had laid afide the plan of building

, a town at Verſoix, in order to eſtabliſh a manufactory there, and to undermine the trade of the people of Geneva, Voltaire determined to do at Ferney what the French government had intended to do at Verſoix.

He embraced the moment of the diſſentions in the republic of Geneva, and by fair promiſes he engaged the exiles to take refuge with him, and many of the malcontents followed them thither.

He cauſed the firſt houſes to be built, and gave them for a perpetual quit-rent; he then lent money, by way of annuities, to thoſe who would build themſelves; to ſome on his own life, to others on the joint lives of himſelf and Madam Denis.

His sole object seemed to me to have been the improvement of this village: that was his motive for asking an exemption from taxes; that was the reason why he endeavoured every day to inveigle workmen from Geneva to establish there a manufactory of clock-making. I do not say that he did not think of money; but I am convinced that it was only a secondary object.

On the two days I saw him, he wore white cloth shoes, white woollen stockings, red breeches, with a night-gown and waistcoat of blue linen flowered and lined with yellow: he had on a grizzle wig with three ties, and over it a silk night-cap embroidered with gold and silver.

Twelve

Twelve years ago he had his tomb built on the fide of his church fronting his houfe. In the church, which is fmall, there is nothing extraordinary, except over the altar, where there is a fingle figure in gilt wood, without a crofs: it is faid to be himfelf; for it is pretended that he always had an idea of founding a religion.

LETTER XXVI.

" YOU would publifh a book," fays La Bruyere; how many critics will fall upon you! You will be called to account for your thoughts, for your phrafes, for your words. " This," you will be told, " is only " proper for converfation; that is only " ufed

"used in the florid style; this other is
"trite; this last is not received: write
"according to the fashion, or do not
"write at all."

Alas! there am I already condemned; I know nothing of the fashion, and I cannot keep from writing *. I cannot give an account either of my phrases, or of my words †; much less of my solecisms and barbarisms: Pardon therefore the style, dear reader, and recollect that in my preamble I

* *Tantus amor scribendi me rapit.*
† I except one only; if an expression in my first page be criticised, I answer that I have used it in its literal sense, that I know no title so glorious for a man as that of *good*; and if the ill-nature and depravity of mankind have annexed other ideas to that word, that is not a reason why it should not be used in its primitive signification. [The reason why the author has defended this expression is, that *bon homme* in French has three significations; it means *a good man, a silly good-natured man*, and *a cuckold*. It is seldom used but in the two latter senses.]

promised

promised you nothing but some ideas and truth.

LETTER XXVII.

Qui se peint tout en beau dans ces lieux qu'il habite,
Méconnoit la nature, et rêve en Sybarite.

He mistakes nature who paints all things bright,
And dreams like a luxurious Sybarite.

THE philosopher of Sans-souci is in the right; and I think I am not mistaken in saying that we ought to look on the fair side as much as we can, because it is for our happiness to do so. I wish that this system were universal, and in order to establish it, I would have every one look for the bright rather than the dark side of an object; the opposite system is that which prevails; a new character

character comes into company, a new book appears, nothing is fought for in them but faults; and if one finds none, one thinks it is a proof of want of wit: I have always thought the contrary; and I think it a more certain proof of wit and taste to discover a single beauty than to point out ten faults. In your travels therefore look always for the beautiful; and when you meet a disagreeable object, turn away your head: I allow you but one exception to this rule; when a beggar presents himself, look upon him; for you can convert into pleasure the pain which the sight of him will give you, by relieving his distress.

Adieu, my dearest friend; I have travelled several years; I have seen many

many men; and the moſt valuable leſſon that I have learned in my travels is this: Different countries have different taſtes, and different ways of thinking on various ſubjects: in one point they all agree, that the beſt letter of recommendation that a man can carry, is a GOOD HEART; and that the fureſt method to make himſelf loved and reſpected every where, is to DO GOOD.

F I N I S.

[173]

many parts, and the most valuable
foftils I have learned in my travels
is this. Different authors have diſ-
courſed, and that with ſigns of
thinking, on variety of ſubjects, too
painfully that it gives this "ſobriety"
of recommendation, that a man
carry, in a good "heart"; and the
[illegible] method to make him [illegible]
loved and reſpected every where
is to do good.

POSTSCRIPT, by the EDITOR.

The Author of thefe Letters may be confidered as a kind of Literary Phænomenon. Mr. Sherlock travels through Italy, and publifhes a book at Rome in Italian. He publifhes another in French at Paris. And it may not be unpleafing to the purchafers of this work to fee accounts of the Author's merits, given by the Journalifts and Reviewers of France and Italy.

1. *Extrait du journal de litterature des fciences & des arts, année* 1780, N° 10.

"Beaucoup d'efprit, beaucoup de gout, des obfervations fines, des vues neuves, de la chaleur & même de la delicateffe: tel eft le caractere de ces

ces Lettres d'un Voyageur Anglois, *qui ont & meritent le plus grand succés.* Un Anglois qui écrit & écrit agréablement en François, est déjà un phénomène capable d'exciter la curiosité. Il est vrai, Monsieur, que notre Nation n'est point en reste de ce côté là, & si M. *Sherlock* se sert de notre Idiôme pour nous faire part de ses observations, les Anglois se rappelleront avec quel succès Voltaire a employé le leur, dans son *Essai sur le poëme epique* & dans l'Epître dedicatoire placée à la tête de *la Henriade.*.

Son style est aisé & a de la grace... ses portraits sont hardis & brillants... l'auteur montre par-tout de la sagacité, du goût & une sensibilité rare. Toutes les fois qu'il parle des arts ou de *Shakespear* son style a de la chaleur & de l'energie... Il y a dans ces lettres des morceaux saillans & des reflexions philosophiques dignes d'un grand ecrivain...

2. *Extrait du journal de Paris. Lundi,* 24 *Avril,* 1780.

" Ces lettres sont écrites avec beaucoup d'agrément & même d' originalité. Elles renferment des observations fines & judicieuses sur les arts, sur les mœurs, sur la litterature. L'auteur semble s'être fait une loi de varier ses sujets &

son

fon ſtyle. Par-tout on reconnoit l'homme d'
eſprit, l'obſervateur, & l'amateur éclairé...
M. Sherlock parle des arts & des talens avec
la chaleur d'un homme qui les juge par la raiſon
& par le ſentiment... Les tableaux qu'il trace
du ciel & de la terre de Naples repréſentent les
couleurs vives & touchantes du modele; & les
remarques ſur les mœurs & ſur l'eſprit des Italiens
ſont aſſaiſonnées de traits heureux & ſaillans...
Il voit en philoſophe, & peint en poëte."

Pour le coup! M. Sherlock ne ſe contente
plus de louer, d'adorer Shakeſpear. Il le defend,
il attaque ſes ennemis; il fond ſur Meſſieurs
de Voltaire et de la Harpe. La renommée du
premier né lui en impoſe pas; la ſévérité du ſecond ne peut l'intimider. *Il juge avec rigueur,*
dit il, *avec rigueur il ſera jugé.*

Ces Nouvelles Lettres feront à coup ſûr aſſez
d'honneur à leur auteur pour qu'il ſe félicite de
les avoir publiées; et au lecteur aſſez de plaiſir
pour qu' après les avoir lues, il ſouhaite de les
relire encore.

3. *Extrait*

3. *Extrait d'une lettre de M. Blin de Sainmore a M. de Sherlock, pour le remercier d'un exemplaire de son livre intitulé,* Lettres d'un Voyageur Anglois.

Journal de Paris, Lundi, 1 *Mai,* 1780.

" Independamment de ce que je vous dois, Monsieur, pour le cadeau dont vous m'avez honoré & pour le plaisir que m'a fait la lecture de votre ouvrage, vous avez encore des droits à ma reconnoissance. Vous rendez justice à ma patrie; votre livre est dedié à un Lord chéri de tous ceux qui le connoissent; vous faites un eloge merité de S. E. Mgr. le cardinal de Bernis, auquel je suis attaché depuis longtems par la réconnoissance; vous appreciez nos grands hommes avec une impartialité peu ordinaire; vous écrivez notre langue avec une *finesse & une grace* qui prouvent que vous vous êtes plu à l'etudier. Je vous prie de croire, Monsieur, que *la justesse* et *la profondeur* de vos observations, ainsi que la *maniere piquante* dont vous les présentez, ne m'ont pas échappé plus qu' à vos autres lecteurs.

J' ai toujours eu une secrette predilection pour votre nation, et ceux que j'en ai connus, n'ont pas peu contribué à me l'inspirer . . . Vous m'annoncez, Monsieur, que vous devez bientôt quitter Paris pour retourner à Londres. Alors vous direz

direz sans doute à vos compatriotes l'accueil obligeant que vous avez reçu des François, malgré la grande querelle qui divise les deux nations. Vous leur direz que par-tout on s'est empressé à vous marquer les égards dus à votre mérite et a rechercher votre amitié."

4. *Extrait du Journal Encyclopédique, Dec.* 1779.

" . . . Il use, on ne peut mieux, du talent Anglois de penser beaucoup en peu de mots, et de parler à l'esprit par abbreviation . . . Il ne faut souvent à M. Sherlock qu'un coup d'œil pour voir et qu'un trait pour peindre . . .

. . . Il semble ici que quelque chose du sublime de l'ouvrage du sculpteur ait passé dans l'ame de l'ecrivain pour se communiquer à son style. Toute cette lettre (Lettre XII.) est en effet admirable.

Nous ne suivrons pas M. Sherlock dans sa marche; mais nous avons trouvé dans chacune de ses lettres une lecture variée et interessante, des pensées fines, des reflexions profondes, un gout delicat, un jugement sain, enfin un esprit excellent, orné de connoissances, un sentiment exquis des arts, le caractere d'une ame honnête, la sage hardiesse d'un amateur instruit, et un style brillant d'imagination, sans qu'elle nuise à la précision des idées . . .   . . . Voilà

… Voilà donc comme s'exprime un etranger dans notre langue, tandis qu'une multitude d'ecrivains nationaux femble confpirer pour la defhonorer par des ouvrage où les fautes de ftyle fourmillent. L'eftime pour M. Sherlock doit encore s'augmenter, fi l'on fe rappelle qu'il ne poffede pas moins heureufement la langue Italienne, comme il l'a prouvé dans un ouvrage écrit à Rome même en cette langue, ouvrage auffi elegant que judicieux, compofé fur les principes d'une faine litterature, et qui feroit encore utile aux jeunes gens qui cultivent la poefie, quand même il ne leur feroit pas neceffaire. Nous ne repeterons point ici les eloges que nous avons donnés à cet excellent ouvrage dans notre journal du 15 Aout dernier. Nous ajouterons feulement, fans croire nous tromper, que M. Sherlock eft le premier Anglois qui fe foit fait connoitre au public par des ouvrages écrits purement dans deux langues etrangeres.

5. *Extrait*

5. *Extrait du Mercure de Mars*, 1780.

Nous avons rendu compte d'un ouvrage écrit en Italien par M. de Sherlock: en voici un qui est écrit en François par le même auteur. *Formas se vertit in omnes.* Mais il a beau changer de forme, on retrouve toujours l'homme d'esprit, l'homme sensible aux beautés des arts, et *presque* toujours l'homme de gout. Ne parlez point de *Shakespear* à M. de Sherlock, & vous le prendrez pour un Elève d'Horace et de Boileau. Les hérésies sont, dit-on, *des opinions de choix*. On ne comprend pas trop comment M. de Sherlock a pu choisir cette opinion, à laquelle il paroit fort attaché. Elle sera pour tous les François à peu-près une heresie enorme, et une opinion qui ne paroîtra pas même d'un choix heureux.

La manière dont cet Anglois écrit tour-a-tour en Italien et en François, paroîtra peutêtre une espèce de phénomène en litterature. Ils sont si rares ceux qui écrivent d'une manière supportable la langue même dans laquelle ils ont appris à sentir et à penser, qu'il suffit sans doute d'écrire deux langues etrangères, aussi bien que M. de Sherlock écrit le François et l'Italien, pour faire preuve d'un mérite très distingué.

Après la lecture des deux ouvrages de M. de Sherlock, nous demeurons perfuadés que lors qu'il ne fera plus obligé de donner aux mots et au ftyle une partie de l'attention, qu'un ecrivain doit donner à fon fujet et à fes idées, que lors qu'il écrira dans fa langue, M. de Sherlock meritera d'être traduit dans toutes les autres. Une chofe bien précieufe que l'on remarque dans ces deux ouvrages, c'eft cette fenfibilité d'un homme de bien, qui ne peut parler fans le plus grand interêt de tout ce qui regarde les vertus et le bonheur de l'homme;

> Et fon ame et fes mœurs empreints dans fes ouvrages,
> N'offrent jamais de lui que de nobles images.

6. *Extrait du Mercure de Mai*, 1780.

Ce qui diftingue fur-tout M. Sherlock de la foule des Voyageurs Ecrivains, c'eft qu'il ne répète jamais ce que d'autres ont dit avant lui. Il rapporte ce qu'il a vu, et il a tout vu avec fes yeux; il écrit ce qu'il a penfé, et il n'a point penfé d'après les autres: par tout il eft lui même. C'eft là ce qui donne à fon ouvrage ce caractere d'originalité, qui, lors qu'il eft accompagné de

la

la raifon et du gout eft *l'empreinte et le fceau du Génie.*

Ne vous attendez pas à trouver dans ces lettres les noms de tous les tableaux fameux ou de toutes les belles ftatues de l'Italie. M. Sherlock a bien fenti qu'une pareille nomenclature (qui d'ailleurs fe trouve par-tout) fatiguoit vainement la mémoire fans intereffer l'efprit, et qu'il y avoit des objets qu'on ne pouvoit voir qu' avec raviffement, et dont on ne pouvoit lire les defcriptions qu' avec ennui. Il a fait un livre et non pas un catalogue. Les chef d'œuvres les plus parfaits font les feuls qui trouvent place dans fes lettres, et il n'en parle jamais qu' avec *une clarte, une grace et une nobleffe,* qui font difparoitre aux yeux du lecteur tout ce que de femblables defcriptions ont pour l'ordinaire de fec et de rébutant. Non content de nous montrer l'ouvrage qu'il veut nous faire connoître, il nous montre dans l'ouvrage le génie de l'Artifte. C'eft ainfi que dans fes prémieres lettres il a peint le génie du fculpteur Grec, par l'Apollon du Belvedere; et c'eft ainfi que dans ce nouveau recueil il nous fait voir dans la *Transfiguration* le génie de Raphael. Ce morceau eft admirable; mais fon étendue nous empêche de le citer, et fa précifion nous ote la poffibilité de l'abréger.

Nous

Nous remarquerons en paſſant que perſonne ne poſſède mieux que M. Sherlock le talent ſi difficile de louer ſans fadeur. Les louanges qui ſortent de ſa plume ſuppoſent une connoiſſance de l'homme et une pénétration ſi parfaites, et ſont exprimées avec une nobleſſe ſi impoſante et un ton de franchiſe ſi perſuaſif, qu'il eſt vrai de dire qu'elles honorent à la fois celui qui les reçoit et celui qui les donne *.

Les nouvelles Lettres du Voyageur Anglois finiſſent par ces mots : " Les prémiers efforts que " j'ai faits pour plaire au public ont été reçus " avec indulgence : ſi celui-ci mérite le même " accueil, je continuerai d'écrire, mais comme " je n'écris que pour la gloire, ſi je ceſſe d'in-" tereſſer, je jette ma plume."

Non, M. Sherlock ; que votre plume reſte encore longtems entre vos mains pour notre inſtruction et pour votre gloire. Continuez d'écrire, et vous continuerez d'intereſſer. Quand, avec des idées neuves et vraies, avec un gout délicat, un taĉt ſûr, un eſprit droit et orné, une imagination brillante, une expreſſion heureuſe, quand avec tous ces avantages on montre encore

* Voyez la Lettre XXXV. ſur M. le Maréchal de Biron, la dedicace à Milord Briſtol, et une note ſur M. l'Abbé de Lageard, Lettre XXIV.

un

un cœur droit et le caractere d'une ame honnête, on peut se flatter de plaire à tout homme qui pense et qui sent, et d'obtenir l'estime & l'admiration des gens de gout et des gens vertueux de toutes les nations et de tous les siecles.

7. *Extrait du Mercure de Fevrier*, 1780.

Le croiroit-on ? M. de Sherlock, qui, dans tout son Ouvrage (*Consiglio ad un giovane poeta*) n'a proposé pour modèle que les poëtes du gout le plus pur et le plus parfait; qui ne parle pas des anciens sans enthousiasme, et qui regarde Boileau comme le guide le plus sûr pour les jeunes poëtes : M. de Sherlock termine son ouvrage par un morceau sur Shakespear, où il place ce poëte audessus des plus beaux génies anciens et modernes. Jusqu'à présent on eût pris M. de Sherlock, a ses opinions pour un François, et à son style, pour un Italien : à peine est il question de Shakespear, qu'on ne peut s'empêcher de lui dire : *Ah! M. de Sherlock vous etes Anglois!*

L'Ouvrage de M. de Sherlock a excité les plus grands mouvemens en Italie; on l'a critiqué avec fureur; on l'a loué avec enthousiasme. L'Abbé Scarpelli termine ainsi un sonnet qu'il

lui

lui a adreffé : " Horace et Boileau, réjouis de
" tes difcours, ont tourné vers nous leurs re-
" gards et fe font écriés : O Italie ! voilà ton
" Longin !" D'autres Litterateurs Italiens l'ont
traité, non feulement comme un homme de mau-
vais gout, mais comme un méchant homme : ils
l'ont traité comme un etranger ennemi qui feroit
allé attaquer Rome dans Rome même. Son
Ouvrage a eu en Italie un fuccès complet.

Pour nous nous penfons qu'un homme qui ré-
pand ainfi des lumières dans les pays où il voyage
pour en acquérir, doit à fon retour, en rapporter
beaucoup dans fa Patrie; et quoique nous nous
foyons permis plufieurs fois de combattre M. de
Sherlock, nous ne doutons pas qu'il ne foit
deftiné à augmenter ce petit nombre d'Ecrivains
Anglois qui ont commencé *à joindre l'elegance
et la régularité du gout, à la hardieffe et à la
profondeur du genie de leur nation.*

Dal

Dal Giudizio dato dall' Efemeridi letterarie di Roma ai N° VIII. IX. e X. dell' anno 1779, full' opera intitolata *Configlio ad un giovane poeta* del Sig. Sherlock.

Amicus Plato, amicus Socrates, fed magis amica veritas.

NON ha potuto l'Autore gettare uno fguardo fulle deliziofe contrade d'Italia fenza efferne penetrato di ammirazione. I fuoi fenfi fono ftati fcoffi dalle opere incantatrici di un Palladio, di un Michelangelo, di un Raffaello: l'immortal Pergolefe ha lufingato il fuo orecchio colla delicata armonìa delle fue note: il celebre Iftoriografo della Repubblica Fiorentina ha rapito il fuo animo; e i voli franchi, e ficuri de' noftri Poeti lirici lo hanno forprefo. Tale diffatti è lo fpettacolo, che l'Italia prefenta agli occhj di ogni culto ftraniero. Ma fpiriti avvezzi ad effer colpiti dalla maeftra profondità, e dalla robuftezza di Pope, di Dryden, di Younck, di Boileau, ed a fentir parlare la ragione fulle labbra di Calliope, e di Euterpe, come fu quelle di Platone, e di Socrate poffono effi piegarfi egualmente ad offerir

degl'

degl' incenfi all' Ippogrifo di Aftolfo, e ad invocare con divota fiducia,

Pape Satan, Pape Satan Aleppe?

...Noi non vogliam difpenfarci dal referire le fue fteffe parole: i noftri lettori ci vorran permettere di allontanarci dalla folita precifione per rapporto ad un'opera, che ha pofto in fermento tutto ill regno poetico Italiano....

La fua Opera ha eccitata una terribile rivoluzione nell' intolleraute repubblica de' noftri Poeti: che ne direbbe Platone, fe foffe al par di noi fpettatore dell' irritabilità, con cui fono accolte fra loro delle verità refe facre; e incontraftabili dal confenfo di tutta la Terra, e fe feriffero i fuoi orecchj come i noftri le grida fediziofe; e confufe, con cui fe ne chiede la più irragionevole vendetta?

...Prima d'inoltrarci a ragionare di effa, è degno di effer riferito il tratto di mafchia eloquenza, con cui il Sig. Sherlock medefimo fi apre la ftrada a parlarne. " Nel momento, dic' egli,
" di una guerra fra l'Inghilterra, e la Francia,
" parrà forfe ftraordinario al mio giovane lettore,
" che io ardifca di fare l'elogio della letteratura
" Francefe. Egli conofce poco i principj della
" mia nazione. Un Inglefe ardifce fempre render
" giuftizia

"giustizia al merito. Quando la sua patria ha
" bisogno del suo consiglio, è pronto a servirla
" con tutti i suo talenti; quando essa ha bisogno
" del suo sangue, è pronto a versarlo fino all'
" ultima goccia; ma nell'istesso tempo, è inca-
" pace di non render giustizia ad un nemico.
" Non v'è una guerra contro le lettere Fran-
" cesi: gli uomini di lettere dovrebbero esser
" compatriotti dappertutto; dovrebbero vivere
" in eterna pace, e render giustizia al merito
" vivo o morto a Londra, a Parigi, a Roma, ad
" Atene." Terribile lezione per gl'Italiani,
niente meno soda, ed opportuna di quelle, che il
Sig. Sherlock ha date loro sulla Poesia, ma forse
vana egualmente!

... In tutte le opinioni del Sig. Sherlock, che
noi abbiamo riferite, vediamo un risultato di una
lunga applicazione, e di un profondo studio
sopra i migliori Autori Greci, Latini, Francesi,
ed Inglesi....

.... Così pensa uno spirito illuminato, così
parla un amico della verità... Chi preferisce il
sentimento alla sterile parola si compiacerà dell'
eloquenza del nostro autore, e gli sarà indulgente
per qualche difetto nella scelta de' termini in
grazia della giustezza delle Idee, e de' vivi tratti
con cui sono dipinte...

La

La Dedicatoria che accompagna questa opera farà una delle poche dedicatorie che saranno lette. Ella è degna di fatti di esser gustata per la precisione con cui è concepita, e per la venustà di cui è sparsa. Speriamo, che i nostri lettori ci sapranno grado di non averli defraudati anche di questa elegante produzione . . .

L'Autore ha consegnato quattrocento esemplari della sua Opera al Libraro Gregorio Settari per vendersi. Il Signor Marchese Maccarani secondando le intenzioni del Signor Sherlock, ha avuto la bontà d'incaricarsi di ricevere il denaro, che ne proverrà, e distribuirlo a povere vedove bisognose. Questo tratto di umanità fa l'elogio del di lui cuore, come l'Opera lo fa del suo spirito.

Translated.

The author has given four hundred copies of this book to the bookseller Gregorio Settari to sell. The Marquis of Maccarani, seconding the intentions of Mr. Sherlock, has had the goodness to charge himself to receive the money, arising from the sale, and to distribute it to poor widows in distress. This trait of humanity speaks as strongly in favour of his heart as the Work does of his talents.

NEW BOOKS.
Lately printed for J. NICHOLS.

British Topography, or an Historical Account of what has been done for illustrating the Topographical Antiquities of Great Britain and Ireland. In two large volumes, quarto. Price Two Guineas and a Half in boards.

A Collection of all the Wills, now known to be extant, of the Kings and Queens of England, Princes and Princesses of Wales, and every Branch of the Blood Royal, from the Reign of William the Conqueror to that of Henry the Seventh exclusive. With explanatory Notes, and a Glossary. Price Eighteen Shillings in boards.

Medals, Coins, Great Seals, and other Works of Thomas Simon; engraved and described by George Vertue. The second edition, with additional plates and notes, and an appendix by the editor. Quarto. Price one guinea in boards.

The Connexion of the Roman, Saxon, and English Coins; deducing the antiquities, customs, and manners of each people to modern times, particularly the origin of feudal tenures, and of Parliaments. Illustrated throughout with critical and historical remarks on various authors, both sacred and prophane. By W. Clarke, A. M. Chancellor of the Church of Chichester. Quarto. Price one guinea in boards.

The History of the Town of Thetford, in the Counties of Norfolk and Suffolk, from the earliest accounts to the present time. By the late Mr. Thomas Martin, of Palgrave, Suffolk, F. A. S. Revised for the Press by Mr. Gough. Quarto. Price in boards 1l. 4s.

Mr. Pegge on the Coins of Cunobelin. 4to. Price 5s. sewed.

Some Account of the Alien Priories, and of such Lands as they are known to have possessed in England and Wales. Two volumes, crown octavo, adorned with a Map of Normandy, and eight other elegant Engravings. Price 7s. sewed.

Four

New Books printed by J. Nichols.

Four new editions of the Supplement to Swift's Works; with explanatory notes on all the former volumes, and an Index, by J. Nichols. In quarto, large octavo, small octavo, and 18mo.—By the affiftance of this Supplement, those who are poffeffed of detached parts of Swift's valuable writings in any fize may compleat their fets, as the latter volumes of every edition may be had feparately.

Ruffia: Or, a Complete Hiftorical Account of all the Nations which compofe that Empire. Two volumes, octavo, price 10s. 6d. in boards. The two concluding volumes will foon be publifhed.

Hymns to the Supreme Being; In imitation of the Eaftern Songs. Octavo. Price 3s. 6d. in boards.

A complete and elegant Edition of the Englifh Poets, in fixty volumes, with Prefaces biographical and critical to each Author, by Samuel Johnfon, LL.D.

A Select Collection of Poems, with Notes Biographical and Hiftorical by J. Nichols. Four volumes, fmall octavo, adorned with portraits by Kneller, Lely, &c. Price 10s. 6d. in boards.—The four concluding volumes, with a general Poetical Index, are in the prefs.

The Original Works of William King, LL.D. Advocate of Doctors Commons, &c. with Memoirs of the Author and Hiftorical Notes by J. Nichols, in three volumes, octavo. Price 10s. 6d. fewed.

The Origin of Printing, in Two Effays, by W. Bowyer and J. Nichols. Octavo. Price 3s. fewed.

The Hiftory of the Royal Abbey of Bec in Normandy, tranflated from a French MS. prefented to Dr. Ducarel by Dom. Bourget. Price 3s. fewed.

Heylin's Help to Englifh Hiftory; continued to the prefent time by Paul Wright, D.D. F.S.A. Adorned with feveral copper-plates. Price 8s. fewed.

Six Old Plays, on which Shakfpeare founded feveral of his Dramatic Writings. Two volumes, crown octavo, price 6s. fewed.

www.ingramcontent.com/pod-product-compliance
Lightning Source LLC
Chambersburg PA
CBHW020903230426
43666CB00008B/1293